Things Shaped in Passing

OTHER PERSEA BOOKS OF INTEREST

More "Poets for Life"
Writing from the AIDS Pandemic

Edited by Michael Klein and Richard McCann

PERSEA BOOKS • NEW YORK

The epigraph is taken from "The Ninth Elegy" by Rainer Maria Rilke,
from **Duino Elegies** by Rainer Maria Rilke, edited and translated by C.F. MacIntyre,
copyright © 1961 by C.F. MacIntyre.
Reprinted by permission of The University of California Press.

Since this page cannot legibly accommodate all copyright notices, pages 207–210
constitute an extension of the copyright page.

Copyright © 1997 by Michael Klein and Richard McCann

PERSEA BOOKS, INC., 171 Madison Avenue, New York, New York 10016

Library of Congress Cataloging-in-Publication Data

Things shaped in passing : more "poets for life" writing from the AIDS pandemic / edited by
Michael Klein and Richard McCann.
    p.   cm.
  ISBN 0-89255-217-4 (pbk. : alk. paper)
  1. AIDS (Disease)—Patients—Poetry. 2. American poetry—20th century. I. Klein,
Michael, 1954 Aug. 17– II. McCann, Richard J.
PS595.A36T45   1996
811'.54080356—dc20   96-4225
                                         CIP

Designed by REM Studio, Inc.
Set in Goudy by Keystrokes, Lenox, Massachusetts
Printed and bound by Haddon Craftsmen, Scranton, Pennsylvania

First Edition

Acknowledgments

The editors wish to express their gratitude to Robert Drake, Marilyn Hacker, Rachel Hadas, B. Michael Hunter, Michele Karlsberg, Jim Marks, David Matias, Eileen Myles, Jerod Santek, Gregg Shapiro, Bridgit Stewart, David Trinidad, Jean Valentine, and Jacqueline Woodson for suggesting poets and for contacting contributors and locating manuscripts; to Elizabeth Alexander and Luis J. Rodriguez for providing an advance manuscript of Melvin Dixon's *Love's Instrument*; to the Fine Arts Work Center in Provincetown for community and support; and to Karen Braziller of Persea Books for her intelligent suggestions and warm counsel.

In addition, Michael Klein wishes to express his gratitude to his colleagues at Sarah Lawrence College, especially Linsey Abrams, Marie Howe, Karen Levey, Tom Lux, Cassandra Medley, and Susan Thames, as well as to his students, for their encouragement and suggestions in the making of this book. Richard McCann wishes to express his gratitude to Mark Doty, Ellen Geist, David Groff, Tony Hoagland, Andrew Holleran, Joanne Jacobson, Jack Pierson, and Richard Sha for their discussion of individual poems and for their conversations about imaginative writing in the age of AIDS; to Vicki Mancuso; Gregory Arms, Nick Flynn, Wesley Gibson, Charlotte Hayes, Karen Kevorkian, Susan Marcisz, Gysbert Menninga, Faye Moskowitz, William O'Sullivan Sky Power, Sarah Priestman, Anne Dabney Richardson, Maxine Rodburg, Tim Rogers, Jane Stanley, and Linda Woolford, whose daily strength and devoted care made life possible; to his students at American University, including Paula Claro, Paul Costello, Michael Nigro, Jennifer Pierson, and Steven Potter, for their thought-provoking analyses of texts in "The Literatures of AIDS"; to Cathy Lee, Elizabeth Lunney, and Robert Scott of the MFA Program in Creative Writing at American University for their assistance with manuscript preparation; to Betty T. Bennett, Ivy Broder, Charles R. Larson, Kermit Moyer, Myra Sklarew, and Henry Taylor, all of American University, for their support; to Carole Horn, M.D., Vinod K. Rustgi, M.D., Timothy Shaver, M.D., V.K. Skaare, R.N., and the staff of Trampani Center of Fairfax Hospital; and, finally, to Gail Hochman of Brandt and Brandt Literary Agency, for her deep warmth and faithful support.

For Melvin Dixon, Tim Dlugos, Lynda Hull, James Merrill,

Paul Monette, Donald W. Woods, and Joel Zizik,

and for Amador Jaime Fernandez

Praise the world to the angel, not the unutterable world;
you cannot astonish him with your glorious feelings;
in the universe, where he feels more sensitively,
you're just a beginner. Therefore, show him the simple
thing that is shaped in passing. . . .
                    . . . And these things that live,
slipping away, understand that you praise them;
transitory themselves, they trust us for rescue,
us, the most transient of all. . . .

—RAINER MARIE RILKE
from "The Ninth Elegy," *Duino Elegies*

Contents

Here, but Differently by Michael Klein   xvii
Introduction by Richard McCann   xix

KIM ADDONIZIO
Metaphors for the Body In Extremis   3
The Weight   4

TOM ANDREWS
From *A Language of Hemophilia*   5

DAVID BERGMAN
The Care and Treatment of Pain   13

RAFAEL CAMPO
El Día de los Muertos   15
The Distant Moon   16
Age 5 Born with AIDS   17
Aida   18

CYRUS CASSELLS
Love Poem with the Wind of Calvary   19
Sung from a Hospice   20

MICHELLE CLIFF
From the Artichoke Capital of the World Namesake of Fidel,
    As In the Queer Part of San Francisco   22

HENRI COLE
40 Days and 40 Nights   25
Carnations   26
The Gondolas   27

ALFRED CORN
Contemporary Culture and the Letter "K"   29

CHRISTOPHER DAVIS
Duende   32
Trying to Flee a Dark Bedroom   33

TORY DENT
   Jade   34
   Future Text Panel   39
   Poem for a Poem   40

MELVIN DIXON
   The Falling Sky   42
   Blood Positive   43
   Wednesday Mourning   43

TIM DLUGOS
   G-9   45
   Parachute   60
   D.O.A.   62

MARK DOTY
   Grosse Fuge   65
   One of the Rooming-Houses of Heaven   70
   Atlantis   71

DENISE DUHAMEL
   David Limieux   82

BEATRIX GATES
   Homeless, Section III from "Triptych"   84

THOM GUNN
   Lament   88
   Memory Unsettled   91
   The J Car   91

MARILYN HACKER
   Against Elegies   93
   Wednesday I.D. Clinic   97

RICHARD HOWARD
   For Matthew Ward, 1951–90   98
   "Man Who Beat Up Homosexuals Reported to Have AIDS Virus"   100

MARIE HOWE
   How Some of It Happened   107
   For Three Days   108

A Certain Light   109
The Promise   110
What the Living Do   111

LYNDA HULL
Suite for Emily   112

MICHAEL KLEIN
After the Disease Concept   124
AIDS, AIDS, AIDS, AIDS, AIDS   125

JOAN LARKIN
Inventory   127
Althea   128
Review   129
Waste Not   130

TIMOTHY LIU
SFO/HIV/JFK   131

DONNA MASINI
Beauty   132

DAVID MATIAS
Some Things Shouldn't Be Written   134
Future Senses   135

RICHARD McCANN
Nights of 1990   137
After You Died   142

JAMES MERRILL
Tony: Ending the Life   143

RON MOHRING
The Useful Machine   147

PAUL MONETTE
Here   149
Manifesto   150
The Bee-Eater   152

MARY JANE NEALON
  Watching the Solar Eclpse with AIDS Patients in
      Infectious Disease Clinic, May 10, 1994   154
  The Illustrious Providence of Solid Tumors   154
  The Pathologist Dictates   155

CARL PHILLIPS
  As from a Quiver of Arrows   157
  Tunnel   158
  From the Devotions   160
  In the Blood, Winnowing   162

BOYER RICKEL
  Poem to Begin the Second Decade of AIDS   165

JEROD SANTEK
  HIV Research Project   167
  Watching "Destry Rides Again"   168

REGINALD SHEPHERD
  Kindertotenlieder   169
  A Plague for Kit Marlowe   170

RICHARD TAYSON
  Blood Test   172
  Peschanka   173
  The End   174
  In Sickness and in Health   176

JEAN VALENTINE
  To the Memory of David Kalstone   178
  The Night of Wally's Service, Wally Said,   178

MAGGIE VALENTINE
  William's Tale: The King of AIDS   179

BELLE WARING
  Baby Random   182
  So What Would You Have Done?   183
  For My Third Cousin Ray John   185

MARVIN K. WHITE
Last Rights   186
That Thing   187

DONALD W. WOODS
Waiting   189

MARK WUNDERLICH
The Bruise of This   193
How I Was Told and Not Told   194

JOEL ZIZIK
Pneumocystis   195
Hmmmm   206

Here, but Differently
Michael Klein

Poets for Life: Seventy-Six Poets Respond to AIDS, the companion anthology to this book, was published in 1989 at a time when AIDS was, for many of its contributors, first entering their consciousness as a literary subject. As writers, the fact of AIDS as an altering experience in the world (and one that was met with a stigma otherworldly in feeling) was the source that many of us drew from. We were sick, or knew people who were sick, and so a kind of elegy for the living and the dead was being constructed line by line. Many of those early poems were grounded in a kind of shock that anything could be expressed at all. When I first wrote poets asking for work, I remember getting a one-sentence letter from Douglas Crase which said, "I haven't begun to find the words."

With the tremor of shock and empathy, they were poems that in the urgency of reporting a crisis were also making discoveries about feelings that had before been uncollected. *How is AIDS giving me the opportunity to function in a new world community?* was the leitmotif that eloquently threaded those poets and their work together to make a book.

The mission is different now. With *Things Shaped in Passing,* Richard McCann and I have made a book unlike *Poets for Life,* but complementary to it—a book that puts that first anthology in an historical perspective and moves on from it, into the landscape of AIDS we now inhabit.

Poetry about AIDS has changed considerably since 1989. While the disease is becoming a chronic, rather than terminal, illness, it has still devastated the world and (as of this writing) a cure is nowhere in sight. I suppose the poems being written today are in some ways more insistent in recognizing AIDS as some enormous aspect of the everyday rather than simply as somebody else's problem.

The motivation for the creation of a second anthology of poems is that some of us are still here. But differently. The poems we received and decided to collect are wide-ranging, but they all seem startled by the same news: being here, but differently. Also distinguishing this anthology from others are the statements accompanying the work. I'm fascinated by some of these statements as much as I am by the poems. I've never heard "apocalypse" attached to this disease before Belle Waring attached it, and it's an eloquent and startling observation. Waring's statement reminds me (without sounding too melodramatic) that this is art for the end of the world. Like Olivier Messian's brilliant *Quartet for the End of Time,* written while the composer was in a concentration camp, these poems had to be written—what Kim Addonizio means when she writes, "I think of the world one human being is, and then all those worlds, gone from this one, and I want never to shut up."

After co-editing *In the Company of My Solitude: American Writing from the AIDS Pandemic,* a book of essays, with Marie Howe, I didn't want to put together another anthology without a pal. I had edited *Poets for Life* alone. It's a lot of work and for this kind of work, this kind of vision, four eyes are better than two. Steadier. Richard

McCann has impeccable taste, an astonishing clarity, and an insight into what would finally become the shape of this book. This anthology is different and yet complements *Poets for Life* because the poetry is marked by the big gesture of the elegist leaving the bedside and looking at the whole fractured world—what that world has become with AIDS in it.

Introduction
Richard McCann

What use was poetry then, those nights, while he sat on the edge of the sofa, fingering the swollen lymph nodes in his neck?

"Don't do that," I told him. "It'll only make it worse."

"It will?" he asked.

I didn't know what to say. He was my partner; he was Jaime. But still I could follow no thought that promised to lead only toward that which seemed unthinkable, as did so much in those days. For instance: Did the word "it" refer to his lymph glands, hardening beneath the soft tissue of his clean-shaven neck? Or did "it" refer to the fear I imagined him broaching each time he touched his glands "obsessively," as if that fretful gesture might somehow release the word—the dreaded word, with its contagious replications—that Mark Doty describes in "Atlantis" as the "vacant/ four-letter cipher/ that draws meanings into itself"?

He touched his neck. I asked him, please, to stop.

To stop *it*. ("I was scared, but not for myself," says the speaker of Belle Waring's "So What Would You Have Done?" And then in the next line, her pained admission: "Of course, for myself.")

One was not yet thinking of Wilfred Owen, who wrote that other than "the monstrous anger of the guns" and the "stuttering rifles' rapid rattle," there would be no "passing-bells" for those "who die as cattle." One was not yet thinking of André Breton, who said that having passed through "the time of fire," the Great War, one could never return to the painting of heiresses and teacups. One was not yet thinking of Anna Akhmatova, who waited "in line outside the prison in Leningrad" during "the terrible years of the Yezhov terror." For the most part, one was thinking only of what one's host had said a few nights before, at a dinner party: "I don't think we need to discuss *that* topic—not here, not in my house." And because one was trying to learn how to live, one wondered: Was he right or wrong to say this? Could he—and he alone, perhaps—speak like this because, as he later reminded us, he'd been the first of us to lose a best friend to AIDS?

Who were we losing then, that night? Afterwards, Jaime sat on the sofa, and I sat beside him, listening to the sound of the air conditioner, with its persistent exhalation. It was barely audible until you listened to it, at which point it entered your head and got stuck there, loud and claustrophobic.

"You don't have AIDS," I told Jaime. "It's not as if you had AIDS. You have ARC." But he had lost his heart for acronymic distinctions.

Here, in this photo, 1985, he is holding the Easter basket I have fashioned, with its "brave flourishes," its "bright and cheerful ribbons." I am standing behind him. Our household of voiceless objects, silences: a white card, noting his next appointment with the doctor, taped to the dresser's beveled mirror; his razor, lying by the sink.

It wasn't that one didn't love language.

One was always searching for a metaphor, although not the kind whose power derives from its having rendered itself as irreducible. One was searching for the kind of metaphor that might control, domesticate. One was always thinking: "waiting for the other shoe to drop."

"I guess that *Poets for Life* is, well, a bit *historical*," one poet said, when I phoned to tell her that Michael Klein and I were seeking submissions for a companion anthology—this anthology—that would complement and deepen *Poets for Life* by presenting extended selections of work by American poets whose language, forms, and purposes have been shaped—and in some cases, in fact, created—by the ongoing experience of the AIDS pandemic, now almost in its third decade.

This is what I told her. And she said, *Yes*, indeed, she had work to send.

But I was still thinking: *Historical? Historical?* The poems in *Poets for Life*—which Carole Muske had described in her introduction as "the stunned words of the bloodied"—seemed hardly "historical," for many of them—such as Olga Broumas's "The Masseuse," Mark Doty's "Tiara," Marilyn Hacker's "Nights of 1965: The Old Reliable," Wayne Koestenbaum's "The Answer Is in the Garden," Michael Lassell's "How to Watch Your Brother Die," and Jean Valentine's "X," among others too numerous to mention—had entered that deep part of the self where the poem creates it own time, and where it begins to carve itself into us, even when it seems to be silent, for it rises again and again into consciousness, often as if unbidden.

But on the other hand: Well, yes, of course it was historical—as what is not these days?

Especially now, in these AIDS years, that is, when time—with its "breathing measuring sweating," as Donald W. Woods writes in his poem "Waiting"—has seemed at once so leaden and so fragmented. Is AIDS-time a viscous suspension? A conflagration? A mechanism of outlandish force, like Henry Adams's dynamo, at last accelerated to the shattering point, with its internal apparatuses now exposed? (Time, as Jaime experienced it: his blue-and-white plastic pill case, beeping in his jacket pocket; his broken travel clock, which ran too fast and couldn't be reset; his occasional, sudden astonishment that he was still alive. In the end, of course, he was "timeless.") How antique and homely seem the old words!—GRID; "exposed to the AIDS virus," or HTLV-III; "co-factors, such as amyl nitrate, or 'poppers'";"five to ten percent of those infected will develop AIDS"; the "miracle cure" of AL-721, an egg lipid, spread on toast. How antique and homely, already tinged with sepia, like one's youth . . .

Especially now, that is, when so many have already died.

If one looks at *Poets for Life: Seventy-Six Respond to AIDS* as an artifact—as, say, what might be construed as a cultural product, created and produced during and against the silences of the Reagan and Bush administrations, and published in 1989—it seems, in a sense, a text equivalent of a benefit performance, with its benedictory preface by the Rt. Rev. Paul Moore, Jr., Bishop of New York ("I have felt moments of grandeur and glory. . . ."); its emotional and crisis-driven foreword by Public Theater producer Joseph Papp ("The ache in my heart is spreading to my chest. . . ."); and its vast and often star-studded cast, many of whose poems are either elegiac or occasional. Moreover, if one considers the book's title as embedded in historical time, one sees how it seems to repudiate—whether by design or accident—the facile linguistic victory of those who claim to be "pro-life," and how, at the same time, it aligns the poems with ACT-UP buttons—SILENCE=DEATH and ACTION=LIFE—to which it adds a new, implied equation: POETRY=ACTION, at least of a kind, for although the poem may seldom possess explicit political power, it does possess the power, as Louise Glück has noted, "to restore avidity." In this same vein, if one considers the subtitle, one sees how it seems to suggest—perhaps unwittingly, with unnamed hope and fear—that AIDS is still situated elsewhere, at a slight remove, as something *other*, and as an entity *to* which one might somehow respond. Is it wrong to imagine the suggestion of a legal metaphor? To imagine AIDS on trial, perhaps, and shackled in the witness stand, facing its angry respondents? One had hoped that AIDS would soon be finalized, like a divorce or an equity case.

What use was poetry then?—as the poem began to forge itself from silences; as it emerged not only in the midst of a viral epidemic but also in the midst of what medical ethicist Paula A. Treichler has termed an "epidemic of significations"; and as it became (as it first was) one's own angered and heartbroken response (if that was ever the right word, the word for which one seemed always to be searching) to what one had begun to experience not as AIDS but as "the AIDS crisis." *Crisis, crisis:* the word that echoed in my head day after day as I first read Paul Monette's poems that were to become *Love Alone: Eighteen Elegies for Rog;* those poems, with their "blood-cries," as Monette called them, and their long chaotic lines insisting themselves into "a howl that never ends." *Crisis:* the word that scared and soothed me, in equal but alternate measures, as if it were the flip side of how I felt myself both terrified and comforted by the isolation of the small Virginia town where Jaime and I then lived.

But in retrospect—looking back at all that has been "shaped in passing," as it were, and looking forward toward that which may still come—one asks if one's sense of the AIDS crisis, at least as a linguistic construction, was not itself a metaphor, necessary to one's own fears and hopes, in that the word "crisis" provided a narrative framework and thus promised the resolution of an experience so overwhelming as to have now shattered the narrative itself. Who now, for instance, could bear the final, beautiful scene of Craig Lucas's *Longtime Companion*, in which the survivors imagine that AIDS is cured and their dead are restored? If our dead were to return to us—in a long procession, say, beneath a silken banner—would they find us marred and hardened from all we have felt and seen in the terrible years since they died? And what would one say to the loved one?—*You did not grow old, as I did. You did not age in my heart, Jaime, as I once hoped you would.*

Certainly the crises continue, day after day, even if their public language is wearied, like the flat phrases that occupy an obituary page, or if their representatives are no longer invited—as they once were, although briefly and then usually as ghouls or pitiable spectacles—on "Geraldo" or "Montel." The crises continue, as they do in Joan Larkin's poem "Inventory," in which the speaker lists her many dead friends, one after another, in a series of interrupted images, but in which she cannot reckon a final accounting, because the whole is not greater than the sum of its parts, and because, more importantly, neither the poem nor the deaths have reached their closures. But who has the heart to live in crisis when crisis drags on and on, as if ceaselessly, so that one might prefer to imagine that one is inured to it, just as one might prefer to imagine one-self inured even to hope? Who has the heart to imagine that AIDS is *only* a crisis, that is, when the crisis has lasted so long as to have become an *event*—an event proportion-al, as psychotherapist Walt Odets writes in *In the Shadow of the Epidemic*, to "the two World Wars and the Great Depression as a psychosocial event of twentieth-century world history."

This is the AIDS that appears most often in *Things Shaped in Passing: More "Poets for Life" Writing from the AIDS Pandemic*—not only the AIDS crisis, *to* which one might respond, but also, and more importantly, the ongoing AIDS pandemic, *from* which one writes and in which the poem becomes not a response but (to borrow lines from Wallace Stevens) "the cry of its occasion,/ Part of the res itself and not about it." This shift in prepositions—not "to" but "from," a shift suggested by the poems themselves—is more than merely grammatical, for the shift in prepositions indicates an ontological shift in one's relation to one's subject, a shift in which the poet serves not as what Terrence Des Pres has called "an *outside* observer distressed by human events" but as an "*inside* par-ticipant." (The conflict between these roles creates both the voice and tone of a num-ber of these poems, such as Rafael Campo's "Aida," Christopher Davis's "Duende," Beatrix Gates's "Homeless," Marilyn Hacker's "Wednesday I.D. Clinic," and Belle Waring's "Baby Random.")

As Mark Doty has said of his own work, in an interview with Michael Klein in *Provincetown Arts*, AIDS has shifted from "*being* a subject"—in the sense of something "apprehended in the distance"—as he now feels it to have been in his poem "Turtle, Swan," which appeared in *Poets for Life*; it has now become, he says, "the dye in which the poem is steeped." Indeed, through the long and ongoing experience of what Doty has called its "corrosive and transforming presence," AIDS has become a critical part of one's "subjectivity," a "great intensifier" that makes everything the epidemic touches "more itself" and that necessitates it be seen not only as personal experience but also as an agent (a "solvent," says Doty) that alters the world and one's most basic relations to it. Certainly the "great intensifier" is repeatedly evidenced in the prose statements we requested from the forty-two poets included in *Things Shaped in Passing*, and which we publish here so that the poets might themselves assess the impress of the AIDS pan-demic upon their imaginations: AIDS often appears, for instance, as a ceaseless "loss of context" (Michelle Cliff) in which "only the present [is] stable" (Tom Andrews), as well as an "apocalypse" (Belle Waring) that has "changed unalterably" not only "our per-spectives on survival" (Marilyn Hacker) but which has in fact changed "everything" (Joan Larkin).

But more important to the purpose of this anthology, the "great intensifier" is evi-denced also within the poems themselves, in which AIDS often serves as the medium through which the world is felt and seen and named. In Marilyn Hacker's "Against Elegies," for instance, AIDS and cancer are perceived together not simply as medical phenomena but as a part of the enormous violence of our century, with its mass deaths and genocides—whether, as the poem notes, in Soweto, El Salvador, Kurdistan, Armenia, Shatila, Baghdad, Hanoi, or Auschwitz—and which therefore "makes every-one living a survivor/ who will, or won't bear witness for the dead." In Lynda Hull's beautiful and feverish "Suite for Emily," the speaker's awareness of her friend Emily—her comrade through "a thousand ruined nights," who is in prison, dying of AIDS, and whom the speaker now addresses, while thinking also of Emily Dickinson—focuses her fierce insistence on this world (with its "tossed gloves & glittering costumes," "its dangerous cobalt luster") as "the only world," even if its mercies are obscured by its "carnivorous streets," its "fabulous breakage," and its "ceaseless *perpetuum mobile*."

In 1994, when Michael and I began to gather these poems for what we then imagined as simply a second volume of *Poets for Life*, we were struck at once by how many of them—such as Tom Andrews's "A Language of Hemophilia," Tory Dent's "Jade," Tim Dlugos's "G-9," Mark Doty's "Atlantis," Beatrix Gates's "Triptych," Richard Howard's " 'Man Who Beat Up Homosexuals Reported to Have AIDS Virus,' " Lynda Hull's "Suite for Emily," Carl Phillips's "In the Blood, Winnowing," Donald W. Woods's "Waiting," and Joel Zizik's "Pneumocystis"—were far longer than most of the poems in *Poets for Life*, the greater number of which were somewhat brief and lyrical. How much has AIDS absorbed into itself, as each day it grows larger?—certainly whole lives, at least, all with their own vast and complicated histories. As it challenges even its own numbed silence and denial, how does the poetic imagination sustain itself as it makes its difficult and sometimes even violent contact with what Wallace Stevens called "the press of the real"? Does it do so, perhaps, by creating its own necessarily hybridized literary tradition?—calling upon Anna Akhmatova, for instance, as does Marie Howe, who achieves an almost religious grace through her Akhmatovian allegiance to detailed sight and simple language; upon Emily Dickinson, with her fierce and intimate knowledge of death, as well as upon Hart Crane's *The Bridge*, and most especially his poem "The Tunnel," with its nightmare vision of urban America, as does Lynda Hull in "Suite for Emily"; upon Constantine P. Cavafy, as does Mark Doty in *My Alexandria*, with its persistent griefs and acute desires; upon Gerard Manley Hopkins, as does Carl Phillips in "A Quiver of Arrows," with its sprung rhythms and its complex syntactical inversions; or upon Frank O'Hara, as does Tim Dlugos in "G-9," with its penchant for New York City gossip and its intelligent and ennobling humor. If these poems assemble a new literary tradition—as might, by extension, *Things Shaped in Passing*—they do so in part by forming what some might see as strange and even impossible imaginative alliances between a homosexual poetic tradition (exemplified by poets such as Whitman, Crane, and O'Hara) and a more expressly political poetic tradition (exemplified by poets such as Akhmatova, Hikmet, Seifert, and Milosz) and by serving as the crossroads on which these poets meet.

These questions and issues—questions and issues posed by the poems themselves—required that we see *Things Shaped in Passing* not only as a companion and sequel to *Poets for Life* but also as a new and separate volume in which the poems evidence an intensified poetic and psychic immersion. We thus wanted to present larger selections of poems by a lesser number of poets than Michael Klein had in *Poets for Life*—for whose contributors, as Michael has noted, AIDS was in many cases "first entering their consciousness as a literary subject"; we wanted the reader to undergo and thus to profit from the psychic immersion that the poems require and that scholar Joseph Cady describes as "disruptive" and "destabilizing." For the most part, we sought to follow this principle in the cases of both established and emerging poets, although we often enough allowed outselves to break it if we felt that a single poem by an author was both greater and more important than our rule.

Some readers will find of course what they feel to be omissions, which result no doubt from our subjective tastes or from what is nothing more than our own occasional ignorance. Although in the end we were able to make available only one-half of the often extraordinary material we gathered, Michael and I were pleased and often even astonished to locate such various and multiple perspectives as are to be had in *Things Shaped in Passing*: the perspectives of those who have contended or now contend with HIV infection, as in (among others) Tory Dent's "Jade," Melvin Dixon's "Wednesday Mourning," Tim Dlugos's "G-9," David Matias's "Some Things Shouldn't Be Written," Paul Monette's "Manifesto," and Donald W. Woods's "Waiting"; the perspectives of family members and lovers, as in Mark Doty's "Atlantis," Marie Howe's "How Some of It Happened," Belle Waring's "For My Third Cousin John Ray," Richard Tayson's "In Sickness and In Health," and Joel Zizik's "Pneumocystis"; the perspectives of those who sought a "drug's good sweep like nothing else," as in Lynda Hull's "Suite for Emily"; the perspectives of dear friends and engaged witnesses, as in Kim Addonizio's "Metaphors for the Body In Extremis," Cyrus Cassells's "Love Song With the Wind of Calvary," and Donna Masini's "Beauty"; the perspective of the hemophiliac investigating the etymology and meaning of his condition, as in Tom Andrews's "The Language of Hemophilia"; and the perspectives of those who are both poets and health care workers, whether as physicians, as in Rafael Campo's "The Distant Moon" and "Age 5 Born with AIDS," or as nurses, as in Belle Waring's "Baby Random" and Mary Jane Nealon's "Watching the Solar Eclipse with AIDS Patients in Infectious Disease Clinic, May 10, 1994," or as volunteer "buddies," as in Maggie Valentine's "William's Tale: The King of AIDS."

But what use was poetry then?—those last nights, while I sat in the hospital beside Jaime, who slept beneath the harsh fluorescent lights that hung above his bed? He had been hospitalized for ascites and liver failure; then he suffered a series of brain seizures and then a stroke.

"Look at me," he said one night. Did he imagine no one could see him? He had been sick a long time. He was often angry, so there were few people left to witness his life. His skin had become so fragile it blistered and bled if anyone touched it. He weighed one hundred pounds.

Then, two nights before he died, his sister flew in from the southwestern city where she lived. It wasn't that she was afraid to come, she explained, though she couldn't say she could agree with her brother's lifestyle. One had to understand that she had wanted to come much earlier, although one had also to understand that she was the person on whom her family depended and who was therefore overtaxed with duties and obligations.

Of course, I thought, *of course*—because she had not once visited, although in retrospect I see that Jaime had kept his life from her at least as much as she had kept herself from it.

We stood on opposite sides of his bed. He was only sometimes conscious. "Jaime," she said. "I'm here. I'm here."

I studied her left eye, which contained a small burst vessel of blood—a hematoma from the airliner's cabin pressure, she said, though it looked like a small red planet consumed by a vivid flame.

Well, I thought, *it serves you right. Your eye has burst with blood because at last it sees what you refused to look upon.* What use was poetry? Her blood-stained eye looked like poetry to me—if poetry were justice.

As it is not, I suspect, unless it is through the justice of its attentive witness, a witness I could not that night provide for her in my anger and my fear. "How much can the eye take in?" asks Donna Masini in her poem "Beauty"; "I think it must be the organ of feeling."

If I were to situate the poems in *Things Shaped in Passing* within a larger context, I would situate a great number within the context of the poetry of witness, in which, as Carolyn Forché describes in her introduction to her anthology, *Against Forgetting,* the poem bears "the impress of extremity," and in which it locates its voice in the space between the realm of "the state and the supposedly safe havens of the personal." Such a poem provides "evidence of what occurred," she writes, but because what occurred now occurs in language, it is also "as much 'about' language as are poems that have no other subject other than language itself." The poem is more than the "trace of an event," says Forché; it is also "*itself* an event"—a "trauma" that one enters through words, "voluntarily," and that "changes both a common language and an individual psyche."

The poem of witness might therefore serve not only as a document but also as a lyrical expression and a protest: as Calvin Bedient has noted, "[T]he lyric can be coarsened and broadened to include the facts." In Paul Monette's "Here," for instance, the elegiac impulse—often regarded as quite "personal," perhaps because of the "overheard" and often epistolary nature of its address—serves not only to protest a lover's individual death ("the only green/ is up by the grave") but also as the foundation for what will become a series of enraged protests, as in his poem "Manifesto," against the social and political forces complicit in the deaths of gay men with AIDS: "the Feds are lying/ about the numbers the money goes for toilet/ seats in bombers the State of the Union/ is pious as Pius washing his hands of Hitler/ Jews are not a Catholic charity when is/ enough enough. . . ." In Marvin K. White's monologic "Last Rights," an angered queen makes comic but defiant protest of the rites of a ex-lover's funeral by claiming his own "rightful place" among those who would deny him any rights at all. In Tory Dent's often surreal and fabulistic "Jade"—a poem of massive ambition, with its extravagant and overheated language "almost passing into chaos," as Whitman once said of his own work—the HIV-positive speaker refuses the ways in which she is perceived (as "contaminated," "a photograph of a dead tree," "a skeletal bride draped in desecrated chiffon") and uses anger as a force through which she can challenge the entire nature and social structure of stigmatization: "Who sent the yellow star swimming in my veins?/ Who plucked it out like an eye and painted it so painfully yellow to begin with?/ / Who stigmatized the pigmentation of my skin?/ Who soaked me in blackness, rain of red and yellow, every inch?"

For Tory Dent, language itself—often stretched to its tearing, and bloated with a strange and new beauty—is a site of resistance, although it is more that, as it is for many of the poets included here, for language is also the means of the poetic imagination's difficult engagement with Wallace Stevens's "pressure of the real"—whether through the sensual, gorgeous, and ultimately transcendent language, say, of Mark Doty's "Atlantis"; the regular measures of Thom Gunn's "Lament"; the anguished but quiet lullaby of Cyrus Cassells's "Love Song with the Wind of Calvary"; the living heart rhythms and "fundamental beating" of Rafael Campo's "El Día de los Muertos"; or the unsentimental and almost brutal diction of Richard Tayson's "The Test." In this sense, the poem is not only "about" the world; it is in fact, as Terrence Des Pres notes in his essay on Stevens in *Praises and Dispraises*, the site on which "imagination and reality meet as equals, and the former draws its character and strength from the latter." Thus, writes Des Pres, "art sustains itself in the world, surviving rushes of negative force that to innocent eyes might seem overwhelming."

In this introduction I have sought to locate the poems that follow within both the context of the AIDS pandemic and the context of imagination and poetry. But of course what I have written constitutes only "some remarks"—remarks that by their nature must be always less than the poems, which bear what Freud would call the "primary process."

What use was poetry? As for me: I worked on this book the last year of Jaime's life. Often I read the poems in his hospital room, while he slept. I read them in the evening, as I sat on the stoop beneath the porch light, petting his dog—*That's a good boy, good boy.* I often read them late into the night. The last week that Jaime lived, I sometimes read them in the afternoon, when I'd retreat from his hospital room to the local swimming pool, where I'd lie on a plasticized chaise longue, listening to Annie Lennox on the Walkman: *No more I love you's. Language is leaving me . . .*

What use was poetry?

It restored me to language. It was equal to life.

The poem stood—with what Stevens called its "nobility " (Stevens, of whom Des Pres wrote: "The real nobility, for this poet, is that despite the strain of pushing back he stays so poised." Words that might have also been said of Tim Dlugos.)

From Lynda Hull, this prayer: "Let her be/ the foam driven before the wind over the lakes,/ over the seas, the powdery glow floating/ the street with evening—saffron, rose, sienna/ bricks, matte gold . . ." From Jean Valentine: "ghost letter." From Cyrus Cassells, a phrase, now committed to memory: "Armorless, open/ To the imperiled . . ."

Sometimes as I read these poems I felt I was an amnesiac returning to his memory. Sometimes I wanted to write down all that Jaime had said, even in what had seemed times of muteness: the shrill rages; the murmured confidences; the ordinary morning greetings; the denials and hopes and angered disappointments; the whispers, still traveling through their catacombs of tenderness and mercy.

September 1996

Things Shaped in Passing

KIM ADDONIZIO

Kim Addonizio, who lives in San Francisco, is the author of The Philosopher's Club, *which received the 1995 Great Lakes Colleges Association Award. "It is difficult to think of just a few sentences that address the relationship between AIDS and my work," she writes. "I could say: It's part of what one sees, if one isn't blind. I could say, like Roethke, 'I, with no rights in this matter,' since my personal griefs over deaths from AIDS are few. I could name former teachers, friends, other writers, strangers, until I'm overwhelmed by the enormity of the loss. I think of the world one human being is, and then all those worlds, gone from this one, and I want never to shut up."*

Metaphors for the Body in Extremis

First I think of it as a factory
where the foreman's passed out drunk
in his high room with the little window
while the radio slides into static
and down below no one gives a shit
about pride in labor considering what they're paid
so one by one they're taking off
their goggles and aprons and building a huge
bonfire in the center of the room and banging
the metal carts against each other while a few
holdouts stay grimly at their tasks
and try to ignore the din. But that's
mechanical and wrong so I close my eyes
to try again: your body is a vase of flowers,
their brown stalks slick in the fetid water,
the shrunken tissue of the petals falling
on a scarred table beside an old couch—
stained, burn-holed—a sunken shape in a darkened
living room. Outside is the worst
section of the city, figures hurrying into doorways,
up to no good, random gunshots and exploding glass,
alarms, alarms—amazing what the mind can do
and still fail to absorb the plain fact
of you, railed-in and dying.
In this nearly sterile room
there are no more ways to imagine
your thin form beneath the covers, your face
I now bend close to kiss,
and whatever I make of the grief
that's coming, it won't change this, *this.*

The Weight

Outside the hospital one afternoon
there was a big, balding man
walking away from the Emergency entrance,

carrying another man in his arms,
past the parking lot booth where a uniformed
guard took someone's ticket and raised

the wooden gate to let the car go,
cradling him as he trudged steadily
up the steep incline to the busy street,

the other man limp, head drifting
against the sweaty shoulder and his thin
arms dangling and swinging. I don't know

if he was still alive, or why they were going
away from help and not towards it.
But I keep remembering how he carried him,

how he paused once and shifted him a little,
the way, if you were a parent, you'd shift
a child to ease the weight, with a kind

of practiced tenderness. I keep seeing such men
all over the city; and I can't help thinking
of Atlas, condemned to shoulder the world,

and Sisyphus shoving at his boulder
that he must have often wished
would simply crush him as it rolled back down.

TOM ANDREWS

Tom Andrews's first collection of poems, The Brother's Country, *was selected for the 1989 National Poetry Series; his second,* The Hemophiliac's Motorcycle, *won the 1993 Iowa Poetry Prize. He teaches at Purdue University. He writes: "As a hemophiliac, I should carry HIV. Statistically, I should. I received many transfusions of Factor VIII during the years when the blood supply was infected. Every adult hemophiliac I had ever met or heard of was infected with HIV. How had I eluded it? When I was convinced I carried HIV, the future narrowed to a point. The past expanded and contracted in waves. Only the present was stable. And the present felt like a continent yet to be explored. I resolved to set out across it, in my work, in my life—to spend my days riotously, wonderingly, intimately, with irrational desire."*

From A Language of Hemophilia

1
Blood pools in a joint
The limb locks

'Acute hemarthrosis'
'Thromboplastin generation'

Hear a language force
Intimacy with
Itself, the world

With and *of*, as in skin's turning
Henna, oxblood, roan, russet

Bruise-blue, color of no jewel

'The secret is locked
    Inside
The structure
    Of the chromosomes'

2
hemo
philia

'blood'
'affection for'

trans
fusion

hema
toma

patho
genesis

anti
body

hyper
trophy

bio
assay

cry
cryo

precipitate
precipice

3

Achtung, says the world. Or was it you. The names of things in chalk on a blackboard. Stars narrow and go out like nothing. The dry in dry ice. The ice in it.

We grow what we can in this soil, some live in attics. The sea is a whale road, the sea is as coarsely gray as itself. Pronouns as 'accrued hieroglyphics'. Leaves take light in sympathy and greed.

Black paint for the swimmers and squirrels tightwalk the wire fence. He would spend a lifetime tracing each passage, each transgression of the word 'the'.

Local color. This is the sign of this. Words
spoken to no one, in particular.
"Those stories, dangerous

toxic waste in Richmond, AIDS discrimination, and celebrity hockey coming up." A friend said, "She seems to really care. For a hematologist, she seems really patient. Really personable."

Stars narrow and. The names of things in chalk
to the smaller midwestern cities
quietly, as if ordered. Go out like nothing. His

sentence moved clockwise, 'native in native time'. Do you think it will rain. The sea.
Black paint. Your eyes find work, there are forms to fill out. Whale road. Wire fence.
Each breath

as it comes as it goes. Arterial
sunrise, capillary dusk. He wanted a listening
speech to approach all things with.

Do you think it will. "She made the disease very understandable and logical." "She
explained all her words."

4
Ooze from a clot, ruined
Tissue

Do you think it will rain

The boy is wrenched from the womb with forceps causing
      a severe hematoma behind the back
Of the skull

Low sounds, the usual questions,
Selfishness transparent as a dog's

Aspirate the knee by extension the page

Firn, cyme, mere, hydrant, okra, bisque

Quoting Freud he said he was
Lived

5
'With these considerations in mind, the objectives of this Workshop on the
Comprehensive Management of Musculoskeletal Disorders in Hemophilia can be stat-
ed briefly as outlined:

1. To bring together knowledgeable people in the field for the exchange of information;

2. To attempt to develop a commonly accepted system of management for the hemo-
philia patient with an orthopedic disability;

3. To develop lines of communication that would serve to foster clinical research in the
field, thus leading to better methods of management;

4. To help disseminate currently available information regarding accepted methods of
management through the publication of the proceedings of this workshop;

5. To encourage the development of additional centers of excellence for the manage-
ment of the hemophiliac patient and his

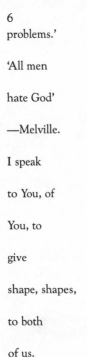

6
problems.'

'All men

hate God'

—Melville.

I speak

to You, of

You, to

give

shape, shapes,

to both

of us.

.   .   .

9
The paramedic on the phone
Teaches; a teacher:

(Oppen: 'a substantial language
Of clarity, and of respect')

"Neck and wrists for Medicalert tag"

"Classical A or von Willebrand's"

"1714 Rolling Hills Circle"

10
'These child-
ren should
not

be
punished, and

their
play with
other

children
should

be super-

vised. If
possible,

they
should have
the

advantages of
a
warm,

dry

climate,

country
life,

and

sea
bath-

ing. Bleed-
ers

with
means

should take
up
some learn-

ed
profession

and, if
they

are
students, duel-

ing
should
be

for-
bidden.'

.   .   .

12
Mother said,
        What you say
of Jesus
        Christ defines

you. End of
        discussion.
Thus I learned
        never to

speak of Him
        or desire
speech. But we
        had 'had words'.

One can break
        silence, but
make it whole?
        'Diagnosis:

Hemoglobin—11.4 gm. per cent
RBC—4.6 million
Platelets—500,000
WBC—12,850
Polys:
        Seg.—36
Lymphocytes—59
Monocytes—4
Eosinophiles—1

Coagulation Studies:

13
Clotting time—40 minutes (normal 5 to 10 minutes)
Clotting retraction—good
Prothrombin consumption—15.5 seconds (normal over 20
        seconds)
Prothrombin time—17.5 seconds (control 14.5 seconds)
Recalcification time—8 minutes (normal less than 180 seconds)
Thromboplastin generation tests with the patient's plasma
and serum and alternately substituting normal plasma and
serum confirmed the diagnosis of classical hemophilia.

14
"We read most of these words and numbers
Uncomprehendingly,
As if they were hieroglyphics"

A day, a day

Recurrences by which
'I' assume

'You'

Thistle, keyhole, spittle, crow

Glide, sample, knot, cheek

'In four years, 84 hemophiliacs have contracted AIDS and 56 have died. A new test to screen donated blood for AIDS virus lowers the risk, but genetically engineered factor VIII should carry no such risk at all and also be much less expensive. Alan Brownstein, the head of the National Hemophilia Foundation, sees the race to produce it as "capitalism at its finest." '

Blood pools in a joint
Hear a language force
Firn, cyme, mere, hydrant

15
The boy pushes a fir twig
through an anthill, flattens
the small cone of dirt.

He studies the ants
escaping, their tiny
hysteria. They rush, weave,

turn and turn. The boy
looks. He looks. Words
are seen to intervene.

. . . .

DAVID BERGMAN

David Bergman is the author or editor of a dozen books, including Cracking the Code, *which won the George Elliston Poetry Prize;* Gaiety Transfigured: Gay Self-Representation in American Literature; *and* The Care and Treatment of Pain. *He lives in Baltimore, Maryland, and is Professor of English at Towson State University. He writes: "The demands that AIDS has placed upon me as a writer have not been whether to talk of it or not, but when can its pain be most forcefully invoked, when does the occasion permit me to speak not in the common public discourse—which is all too easy and sentimental in its anger, far too suspect as a political commodity—but in a language that will fit the dignity of those I have loved who have died."*

The Care and Treatment of Pain

In memory of Allen Barnett

I came to learn what the well can learn
from the dying and the gravely sick:
the fine art of living with the quick
unknitting of flesh. Tired and gaunt,
he faced me across the small banquette
and spoke as rare and welcomed rains
steamed up, like smoke from a cigarette,
the dark windows of the restaurant.

"See these bubbles rising from my head,
purple cancers 'winking at the brim'
which nothing's stopped, not even a grim
experiment with interferon
shot straight into my tumorous scalp.
So far the only result has been
I can find how far the lesions spread
by counting the needles going in.

Yet by the eighth I seem to lose track,
and at the tenth, I begin to curse
and not to myself. Meanwhile the nurse
continuing work without a pause,
reserves her comments until she's through:
'This wasn't so bad. It hardly hurt.
You need a positive attitude.'
Then leaves me listening to her skirt

rustle down the antiseptic hall.
I'm free to go. I gather my things,

coat and hat and a lampshade I brought
for a friend even sicker than I
who can't get out and lives nearby.
But on the street when I feel the sting
of the wind pushing me to the wall,
I allow myself the chance to cry,

this once to luxuriate in pain,
to bathe myself in the swirling tide
of the purest grief and then to ride
out agony so that I can reach
what has always stood on the other side:
a hopelessness that is not despair,
but a truth meant to bring me no where
except to myself and to this time.

And there I am in the busy street
surrounded by those who do not care
whether I'm to live, or how, or where
as long as I ask nothing of them.
They turn as I stagger on my feet,
a joke that can't even force a groan,
a drunken reveler who stands alone,
his humorless lampshade in his hand.

If now it seems I have only pain
to remind me that my life is real,
I mention it not as an appeal
for sympathy or understanding,
rather from a wish to make it plain
that it's earned a certain tender love
that I used to give to other things
which now I have no desire of."

He smiled at me—the lesson done.
and grabbed the tab and rose from his seat,
"Next time," he said, "it'll be your treat,
that is if there'll be another one."
He took from the rack his coat and hat,
a half-read book and a hand-carved cane,
and throwing a kiss to where I sat,
walked out through the cool Manhattan rain.

Easter Sunday, 1991

RAFAEL CAMPO

The son of a Cuban immigrant father and an Italian-American mother, Rafael Campo is a graduate of Amherst College and Harvard Medical School. He currently practices medicine at Boston's Beth Israel Hospital, where he works with people with AIDS and the indigent. He is the author of two collections of poems, What the Body Told *and* The Other Man Was Me, *which was selected for the 1993 National Poetry Series, and a collection of essays,* The Poetry of Healing. *In "AIDS and the Poetry of Healing," he writes: "So-called formal poetry holds the most appeal to me because in it are present the fundamental beating contents of the body at peace: the regularity of resting brainwave activity in contrast to the disorganized spiking of a seizure, the gentle ebb and flow of breathing, or sobbing, in contrast to the harsh spasmodic cough, the single-voiced ringing chant of a slogan at an ACT UP rally in contrast to the indecipherable rumblings on the Senate floor. The poem is a physical process, is bodily exercise: rhymes become the mental resting places in the ascending rhythmic stairway of memory. The poem perhaps is an idealization, or a dream of the physical—the imagined healthy form. Yet it does not renounce illness; rather, it reinterprets it as the beginning point for healing."*

El Día de los Muertos

In Mexico, I met myself one day
Along the side of someone's private road.
I recognized the longing in my face,
I felt the heavy burden of the load
I carried. Mexico, I thought, was strange
And very dry. The private road belonged
To friends more powerful than I, enraged
But noble people who like me sang songs
In honor of the dead. In Mexico,
Tradition is as heavy as the sun.
I stared into my eyes. Some years ago,
I told myself, I met a handsome man
Who thought that I was Mexican. The weight
Of some enormous pain, unspeakable
Yet plain, was in his eyes; his shirt was white,
So white it blinded me. After it all
Became more clear, and we were making love
Beneath the cool sheet of the moon, I knew
We were alive. The tiny stars above
Seemed strange and very far. A dry wind blew.
I gave myself to him, and then I asked
Respectfully if I might touch his face.
I did not want to die. His love unmasked,
I saw that I had slept not with disgrace
But with desire. Along the desert road,

A cactus bloomed. As water filled my eyes,
I sang a song in honor of the dead.
They came for me. My grief was like a vise,
And in my blood I felt the virus teem.
My noble friends abandoned me beside
The road. The sun, awakened from its dream,
Rose suddenly. I watched it as I died,
And felt the heaviness of all its gold.
I listened for the singing in the distance.
A man walked toward me. The story he told
Seemed so familiar, pained, and so insistent,
I wished I would live long enough to hear
Its end. This man was very kind to me.
He kissed me, gave me water, held me near.
In Mexico, they sing so exquisitely.

The Distant Moon

I.

Admitted to the hospital again.
The second bout of pneumocystis back
In January almost killed him; then,
He'd sworn to us he'd die at home. He baked
Us cookies, which the student wouldn't eat,
Before he left—the kitchen on 5A
Is small, but serviceable and neat.
He told me stories: Richard Gere was gay
And sleeping with a friend of his, and AIDS
Was an elaborate conspiracy
Effected by the government. He stayed
Four weeks. He lost his sight to CMV.

II.

One day, I drew his blood, and while I did
He laughed, and said I was his girlfriend now.
His blood-brother. "Vampire-slut," he cried,
"You'll make me live forever!" Wrinkled brows
Were all I managed in reply. I know
I'm drowning in his blood, his purple blood.
I filled my seven tubes; the warmth was slow
To leave them, pressed inside my palm. I'm sad
Because he doesn't see my face. Because

I can't identify with him. I hate
The fact that he's my age, and that across
My skin he's there, my blood-brother, my mate.

III.
He said I was too nice, and after all
If Jody Foster was a lesbian,
Then doctors could be queer. Residual
Guilts tingled down my spine. "OK, I'm done,"
I said as I withdrew the needle from
His back, and pressed. The CSF was clear;
I never answered him. That spot was framed
In sterile, paper drapes. He was so near
Death, telling him seemed pointless. Then, he died.
Unrecognizable to anyone
But me, he left my needles deep inside
His joking heart. An autopsy was done.

IV.
I'd read to him at night. His horoscope,
The New York Times, The Advocate;
Some lines by Richard Howard gave us hope.
A quiet hospital is infinite,
The polished, ice-white floors, the darkened halls
That lead to almost anywhere, to death
Or ghostly, lighted Coke machines. I call
To him one night, at home, asleep. His breath,
I dreamed, had filled my lungs—his lips, my lips
Had touched. I felt as though I'd touched a shrine.
Not disrespectfully, but in some lapse
Of concentration. In a mirror shines

The distant moon.

Age 5 Born with AIDS

In Jaime's picture of the world, a heart
As big South America shines out,
The center of the only ocean. Three
Stick figures (one is labelled "me") are drawn
Beside the world as if such suffering
Could make us more objective. Jaime's bald

And has no mouth; his parents aren't like him,
They're all red lips and crazy yellow hair
And grins. There is no title for his work
Of art, except the names we give ourselves.

Aida

I've never met the guy next door. I know
He's in there—mud-caked shoes outside to dry,
The early evening opera, the glow
(Of candlelight?) his window trades for night—

I think he's ill, since once the pharmacy
Delivered his prescriptions to my door:
Acyclovir, Dilantin, AZT.
He doesn't go out running anymore.

I've heard that he's a stockbroker who cheats
A little on his taxes. Not in love,
They say—he seems to live alone. I eat
My dinner hovering above my stove,

And wondering. Why haven't we at least
Exchanged a terse hello, or shaken hands?
What reasons for the candlelight? His feet,
I'm guessing by his shoes, are small; I can't

Imagine more. I'd like to meet him, once—
Outside, without apartments, questions, shoes.

I'd say that I'm in love with loneliness.
I'd sing like candlelight, I'd sing the blues

Until we'd finished all the strawberries.
We've never met, and yet I'm sure his eyes
Are generous, alive, like poetry
But melting, brimming with the tears he cries

For all of us: Aida, me, himself,
All lovers who may never meet. My wall—
As infinite and kind-faced as the wealth
Of sharing candlelight—it falls, it falls.

CYRUS CASSELLS

Cyrus Cassells lives in Rome, Italy. He is the author of The Mud Actor, *which was selected for the 1982 National Poetry Series, and* Soul Make a Path Through Shouting, *which Rita Dove described as "the most spectacular book I've seen in years," and which received the Poetry Society of America's William Carlos Williams Award. "I think we need to acknowledge as people, and as poets," he writes, "that our hearts have been ripped out by this crisis, this vast 'simoon of contagion,' and that from this devastated place, we will have to fashion a truer art, a new world, where only active compassion, humility, and here-and-now love will do."*

Love Poem with the Wind of Calvary

Rosso Fiorentino's *Deposition from the Cross*

My love, all season I've stared
at Rosso Fiorentino's pallid
saviour and son,
the unstinting arms, the windswept
garments of his followers,
as they clasp
the marionette-inert body—
green limbs, green limbs—
the Renaissance painter's palette
harrowing, immediate,
his altarpiece suffused
with helplessness,
as if this happened here today:
the adder-cold ladders
of mourning,
Mary, pierced-to-the-quick—
who in his hubris would unmake
a woman's labor?—
and the magdalen, a carmine
flare at the base of the cross,
a carmine pleading:
no, not this—

Unbearable knowledge, the desolating
wind in the hospice:
*now the disease has seeped
through the blood-brain barrier,*
and our friend murmuring,
plague-wracked, gallant,
jettisoned-from-youth:

I am not disease only;
hold me as you would hold
the body of Christ—

Love, love, here are my lids,
fragile as leafdrift,
my flesh, mortal
to the infinite power;
against Time's ruffian wind,
for all our days remaining,
hold me as you would hold
the body of Christ—

Tell the lightning-struck,
inconsolable apostle
turning away
from his sapless king
in lush tears,
in lingering reverence—
how do I serve
this dead young man?—
love's a soul-jolting majesty,
love's a make-do
ladder to grief:
finger-warm pledges,
and green limbs, green limbs . . .

Sung from a Hospice

Still craving a robust
Tenderness and justice,
I will go on living
With all I have seen:
Young men lusterless;
Against my blind cheek—
Blessed be the frangible
And dying,
The irreplaceable dead—
In my crestfallen arms:
With breath,
Then without it,
With flesh,
Then freed of it—

And the indurate man I heard
Condemn the stricken,
While my cousin was dying,
If he had walked these wards,
Armorless, open
To the imperiled,
Surely he would have gleaned
To sit in judgment
Is to sit in hell—

Lesions, elegies,
Disconnected phones—

Rain, nimble rain,
Be anodyne,
Anoint me
When I say outright:
In the plague time, my heart
Was tested,
My living soul
Struck like a tower bell,
Once, twice,
Four times in a single season.

MICHELLE CLIFF

Michelle Cliff is Allan K. Smith Professor of English Language and Literature at Trinity College, in Hartford, Connecticut. She is the author of three novels, including No Telephone to Heaven *and* Free Enterprise; *a collection of stories,* Bodies of Water; *and two volumes of poetry,* The Land of Look Behind *and* Claiming an Identity They Taught Me to Despise. *She writes: "I thought at first, as I imagine others have, that soon we'd all be called back into the living room and be told the parlor game was over. The experience of AIDS for me has been a loss of context. Of people like the writer Arturo Islas and the painter David Vereano with whom I felt an instant, sharp kinship. David and I spent hours talking about being child-immigrants to the United States; he, a Jew from Egypt, me, a Jamaican. The experience of AIDS has been for me a growing fury."*

From the Artichoke Capital of the World Namesake of Fidel, As In the Queer Part of San Francisco

I
Vito said that without
us
American culture would be "Let's Make a Deal"

Let us now praise famous queers.

II
Last night I danced *salsa* till 1 A.M.
and came home smelling like a queen—
Opium or Charlie in my hair.

Driving home on 1
empty
half-moon hanging over the ocean,
Pacific,
landscape where herons sleep
turtles call out in dreamtime
where by day
day by day fields know
the comeback of the short-handled hoe.
Strawberries, artichokes, lettuce,
everything is close to the ground.

III
But last night!
Last night, my dear
Las jotas!
And me, *una tortillera* in magenta silk—
you like to know these things.

The band-singer
voice smoked
raked over time
with romance of cigarettes
and scotch—
La estrella, a woman explains to me
La estrella, seated between her mother
and her lover.

Francine, *nacido* Francisco,
bitch in two tongues
mistress of ceremonies,
demanding *aplauso!*
for Victoria, Alexis
Madonna, dollars tucked into their bras.

In a room where a silvery world
turns above us
and the face we know better than our own—
not *La Virgen de Guadelupe, Madre de las Americas,*
not Frida, of the wingéd eyebrows, Trotskyite
not Rita, Gilda, *una Chicana nacido Margarita Cansino*
whose father fucked her to sleep every night—
but Marilyn, whose visage graces the room
platinum and sweet.

IV
A slender boy-bodied farmworker
asks me to dance.
He is in debt to coyotes
He works the fields within spitting distance
of the bar.
His legs fall asleep
and he rubs them with a boyish hand
and smiles with his head bowed.

V
The morning you died
a piece of blue glass
fell out of the sky
from the beak of a bird.

VI
Vito and I decided that when it's all over
said and done—as they say
we become light.
Last night I dreamed my little gray cat
with the sweetest balls you ever saw,
who was killed last week,
had become a constellation—
each yellow eye a supernova.

Every queer I've ever known loved the stars.

HENRI COLE

Henri Cole is the author of three collections of poetry, The Marble Queen, The Zoo Wheel of Knowledge, *and, most recently,* The Look of Things. *He was the 1995–96 recipient of the Rome Prize of the American Academy of Arts and Letters, and he is currently the Briggs-Copeland Lecturer in Poetry at Harvard University. "I do not know if my poetry has been changed by AIDS," he writes. "But my life has. Because I am an autobiographical poet, one is a lake feeding the other. Death, like sexuality and faith, envelops us the way the diver is enveloped by the sea. It is not a question of being 'affected by AIDS.' It is a question of turbulent intimate conversions."*

40 Days and 40 Nights

Opening a vein he called my radial,
the phlebotomist introduced himself as Angel.
Since the counseling it had been ten days
of deep inversion—self-recrimination weighed
against regret, those useless emotions.
Now there would be thirty more enduring the notion
of some self-made doom foretold in the palm.

Waiting for blood work with aristocratic calm,
big expectant mothers from Spanish Harlem
appeared cut-out, as if Matisse had conceived them.
Their bright smocks ruffling like plumage before the fan,
they might themselves have been angels, come by land.

Consent and disclosure signed away, liquid gold
of urine glimmering in a plastic cup, threshold
of last doubt crossed, the red fluid was drawn
in a steady hematic ooze from my arm.
"Now, darling, the body doesn't lie," Angel said.
DNA and enzymes and antigens in his head
true as lines in the face in the mirror
on his desk.

      I smiled, pretending to be cheered.
In the way that some become aware of God
when they cease becoming overawed
with themselves, no less than the artist concealed
behind the surface of whatever object or felt
words he builds, so I in my first week
of waiting let the self be displaced by each

day's simplest events, letting them speak
with emblematic voices that might teach me.
They did . . . until I happened on the card
from the clinic, black-framed as a graveyard.
Could the code 12 22 90 have represented
some near time, December 22, 1990, for repentance?
The second week I believed it. The fourth I
rejected it and much else loved, until the eyes
teared those last days and the lab phoned.

Back at the clinic—someone's cheap cologne,
Sunday lamb yet on the tongue, the mind cool as a pitcher
of milk, a woman's knitting needles aflutter,
Angel's hand in mind—I watched the verdict-lips move,
rubbed my arm, which, once pricked, had tingled then bruised.

Carnations

At the pool he writes
letters in the shade.
There is little news to report.
Overhead Judas trees
shed red petals.
The air is scented
with body lotion.
Bathers with blue lips
shiver in the spring water.
Three guards with silver
crosses at their throats
are playing cards
in a shaft of light.
The prognosis is not good.
But what a sight he is!—
digging into a basket
of raspberries.
The briny bottled water
soothes his eroded mouth
as he speaks of his boyhood,
which was not so long ago,
in the corn fields of Illinois.
After strolling through
the ancient quarter,

he is out of breath,
so we sit beneath a plane tree
which is like a big stone church
in whose dark murals
I see that I will lose him.
If only I could say Go back! Go back!
As in Delacroix's
little masterpiece
where a Natchez child
is born in haste
on a bend of the Mississippi.
The young parents—
he in feathered headdress
and she but a necklace
of orange and green beads—
had been fleeing an army
when the labor pains began.
If only I could run a black comb
through the fatigued mother's
black hair and warn them,
You must go back!
But the little shallop,
awaiting their flight upriver,
stays parked in sand.
The sky, as if flesh,
grows black and blue.
Art, like life, is pitiless.
It is All Saints' Day.
Flower vendors are selling
carnations to adorn the dead.
Far off, an ambulance
wails on the horizon.

The Gondolas

It has been so long since he left his country
that he cannot remember its face.
At the arena for athletes nobody sees what he is thinking.
Christopher Columbus, at the stadium gates, points to the New World.
A dozen perfect crystallizations of flesh sprint on the field.
Above them gondolas dangle from a cable
rising to the mountaintop.

It has been so long since the illness that he cannot remember
what drew him from the prairie.
What he hears is not Miguel sailing through the porcelain sky,
hollering for him like the archangel,
but the battered past,
the years of implacable longing so long ago
in parks and darkened rooms where others like him were known to go.
"Let this be clear," a voice in immaculate speech is saying,
"This man loved earth, not heaven, enough to die."
And the Ferris wheel by the sea rolled over and over,
no less than the sea itself
pummelling Columbus's three little ships,
trying and trying to be lifted by it.

ALFRED CORN

Alfred Corn is the author of seven collections of poetry, including Notes from a Child of Paradise *and* Autobiographies, *as well as the author of* The Metamorphoses of Metaphor, *a collection of critical essays. He lives in New York City, where he teaches in the Graduate Writing Program at Columbia University. "One way my life as a poet can be divided is B.A. and A.A.—Before AIDS and After," he writes. "My collection* The West Door *is dedicated to my dear friend, the critic David Kalstone, who died of AIDS-related illness before the book was published. I was in the very room where David died; I heard his very last breath. Since then there have been close to thirty other friends struck down by the same illness, a figure engraved in consciousness after I recently made a list of names in order to read them as part of the commemoration of World AIDS Day at the Cathedral of St. John the Divine in New York City. Meanwhile, many other friends are living right now with HIV and AIDS-related illnesses. My hope of never contracting the virus is blended with a determination not to sit idly by while others suffer. A secret longing I have never confessed before now is that some of the things I write might be read by those in the valley of the shadow and found helpful. And I have a further hope: that the extraordinary writing about AIDS we've seen over the past decade will make a difference in how people with AIDS are regarded and assisted."*

Contemporary Culture and the Letter "K"

First inroads were made in our 19-aughts
(Foreshadowed during the last century by nothing
More central than "Kubla Khan," Kipling, Greek
Letter societies, including the grotesque KKK—
Plus the kiwi, koala, and kookaburra from Down Under)
When certain women applied to their moist eyelids
A substance pronounced *coal* but spelled *kohl*,
Much of the effect captured on Kodak film
With results on and off camera now notorious.
They were followed and sometimes chased by a platoon
Of helmeted cutups styled the *Keystone Kops*, who'd
Freeze in the balletic pose of the letter itself,
Left arm on hip, leg pointed back at an angle,
Waiting under klieg lights next a worried kiosk
To put the kibosh on Knickerbocker misbehavior.
Long gone, they couldn't help when that hirsute royal
King Kong arrived to make a desperate last stand,
Clinging from the Empire State, swatting at biplanes,
Fay Wray fainting away in his leathern palm
As in the grip of African might. Next, marketing
Stepped up with menthol tobacco and the brand name
Kool, smoked presumably by models and archetypes

Superior in every way to Jukes and Kallikaks.
By then the race was on, if only because
Of German *Kultur*'s increasing newsworthiness
On the international front. The nation that had canned
Its Kaiser went on to sponsor debuts for the hero
Of *Mein Kampf*, Wotan of his day, launching thunderbolts
And Stukas, along with a new social order astonishing
In its industrial efficiency. His annexing
Of Bohemia cannot have been spurred by reflecting
That after all Prague had sheltered the creator
And in some sense alter-ego of Josef K.,
Whose trial remained a local fact until the fall
Of the Empire of a Thousand Years, unheard of in "Amerika"
Of the Jazz Age. But musicians Bix Beiderbecke and Duke
Ellington somehow always took care to include the token
Grapheme in their names, for which precaution fans
Of certain priceless '78s can only be grateful.
They skipped and rippled through a long post-war glow
Still luminous in the memory of whoever recalls
Krazy Kat, Kleenex, Deborah Kerr, Korea, Kool-Aid,
And Jack Kennedy. Small wonder if New York had
A special feeling for the theme, considering radical
Innovations of De Kooning, Kline, and Rothko. This last
Can remind us that bearers of the letter often suffered
Bereavement and despair (*cf.* Chester Kallman) and even,
As with Weldon Kees, self-slaying. Impossible not to see
Symptoms of a malaise more widespread still in a culture
That collects kitsch and Krugerrands, with a just-kids lifestyle
Whose central shrine is the shopping mall—K-Mart, hail to thee!
To "Kuntry Kitchen," "Kanine Kennels," and a host of other
Kreative misspellings kreeping through the korpus
Of kontemporary lingo like an illness someone someday
(The trespass of metaphor) is going to spell "kancer."

True, there have been recidivists in opposite
Direction (a falling away perhaps from the Platonic ideal
Of *tò kalón**) like "calisthenics" and Maria Callas,
Who seem to have preferred the less marblelike romance
Of traditional English. This and related factors make all
Supporters of the letter "k" in legitimate forms
And avatars cherish it with fiery intensity—

*tò kalón: Greek, "the beautiful"

All the more when besieged by forces beyond
Anyone's control, at least, with social or medical
Remedies now available. Dr. Kaposi named it,
That sarcoma earmarking a mortal syndrome thus far
Incurable and spreading overland like acid rain.
A sense of helplessness is not in the repertory
Of our national consciousness, we have no aptitude
For standing by as chill winds rise, the shadows gather,
And gray light glides into the room where a seated figure
Has taken up his post by the window, facing away from us,
No longer bothering to speak, his mind at one with whatever
Is beyond the ordinary spell of language, whatever dreams us
Into that placeless place, its nearest image a cloudless
Sky at dusk, just before the slow ascent of the moon.

CHRISTOPHER DAVIS

Christopher Davis is the author of The Tyrant of the Past and the Slave of the Future, *which won the 1988 Associated Writing Program Award. Born in Whittier, California, he now lives in Charlotte, North Carolina, where he teaches at the University of North Carolina. He writes: "The slow, inert, emotionally conservative atmosphere of a white-collar Southern city threatens me slightly, because it pushes back against the extreme restlessness in me, but the tensions between inner and outer possibilities can be a source for poetry as much as simpler, unrestrained exuberance. In 1992, I organized an off-campus creative writing project for people with HIV: in part because the project could not be supported by either the local academic or gay communities, it folded, but not before one gentleman wrote over a dozen strong, desperate poems. He appears in 'Duende.' "*

Duende

One swollen evening,
warm rain flooded the gutters.
Dogwood blossoms had come out
over a wash of green leaves.
The world seemed quietly willing.
After a late, stiff lunch,
I lay back
and let a sick man
tenderize me, licking
my shoulder blades, my navel, my ass-
hole, opening
my body's envelope,
consuming the glue,
sheating my flesh opener
inside his cheeks.
Waiflike, I prayed,
"Do you think it's all right,
your saliva?" "I think so," he smiled.
"Don't do something you don't want to do."
I touched his bald spot.
From his cock tip,
ghostly honey
oozed slowly
to the white shroud.
My white teardrop
plopped on my navel,
a pear tree petal
pressed to a wet windshield.

Rain throbbed on the roof.
Minutes throbbed on.
He handed me a poem about a rotting dog.
He brought me back. I collapsed
onto this green, bacon-scented sofa,
happy for a moment, wrapped
inside this stinking orb.
I puffed some grass.
Minutes pulsed past.
I felt like a dead bass
flopped out onto the sidewalk,
scales baked to a steel-gray leather
in the sun, a pelt of ants swirling
around me, nipping me, driving
me nuts, tucking
me in, my body
less strong than the mind,
the world around us suddenly
so young.

Trying to Flee a Dark Bedroom

We could
have death, turning on
a see-through globe's lightbulb, our small reach
expanding over contoured
continents. Rubbed between fingertips, the Andes.
The spine's gone. Then the Rockies. Nevada's desert, glowing
red around this palm, feels
like sun-crumpled leather. Maybe it is
all overheating
from the core out. This afternoon, late, the heat needled
a private's dust-brown back
until he squirmed, naked, boring
down into
the rough, dry grass, nailing
a hunger burned by ants
into a grave's eye.
Failing to.

TORY DENT

Tory Dent is the author of What Silence Equals, *which Sharon Olds describes as "a prayer for
the creation of meaning, for an emergency of art equal to the emergency of life." "There is a dan-
ger in romanticizing AIDS by focusing too much on the art produced by it," Dent writes. "The
emphasis needs always to be on the disease—art is only its representation, and inherently false
as such. Life comes before art and AIDS ends life."*

Jade

Upon a plain of thought, a box,
Ornate as a medieval bodice.

Within the box, another box: the renaissance of jeweled boxes.

Dissecting the boxes with surgical gloves,
A blond and bright nothingness,
You watch the descent to smallness, once in love with diminutiveness.
Box within box within box within box. . . .
Centuries stripped raw, poignantly.

In the very last box (if there is one), this century,
The root of the problem displayed upon velvet
Like the Nairobi diamond or Nairobi itself.
A Haitian pufferfish in its embalmed perfection;
Desire frozen with moribund deception. O so artfully.

Wrapped in plastic, the dormant heart,
"Ti bon ange" trapped in a jar,
Still feathers against what makes up the glass,
Your fear which makes it impenetrable,
Sentences me temporarily to a bell jar like Juliet.

In the very last box (if there is one), this evening,
Marbleized by the moonlight and vaulted like a ceiling.
You and I sit on a sofa, a turbulent dinghy.
You're afraid to kiss me, the plot of our first kiss,
The backdrop, foiling us.
"Do you think of me as contaminated?" I ask you finally.
"I think of you as a beautiful jeweled box," you reply very quietly,
"And inside you is a box even more beautiful."

But in your eyes I interface myself,

A photograph of a dead tree
Or a painting of a living tree.
That minute carnelian buds have begun there makes no difference.
One can easily turn away from a photograph or a painting.

I see the dirt pile up in the distance,
Dug up by the tiny spoon that doles out the pufferfish powder.
Someone left a jar of it outside my house.
And in the very last box (if there is one), inside me
Lies the spoon raised on velvet, a corpse in its tomb.

It swallows up everything I am, this box.
This box a blood test, this box, an abstraction,
This box a coffin of sorts
That buries inside my body the antibody HIV;
My body's counterbody, the proof, nonproof,
A footprint, this root, merely a photograph of a root,
A photograph of a dead tree.
This origin, a nonorigin mistaken for the truth
Devours me almost cannibalistically
To a skeletal bride draped in desecrated chiffon, once white.
Coffin within coffin within coffin within coffin. . . .
Within my body, a pilgrimage of candles floats.
Within my body, a coffin burns in the snow.
My soul, a firefly the witch doctor now owns,
A flaming boat, my sinewy hold on myself, a tiny angel,
Pinned like a collected butterfly,
Anesthetized by the powder mixed from pufferfish and skull
The Haitian witch doctor grinds to pharmaceutical dust.
Someone blew a cloud of it into my face,
A desert storm where your parents live.
The powdery sand seeps from my skin to my brain.
"They call it the Romeo and Juliet drug," you said,
Ordering all my orifices to be closed
By martial law your peers enforced,
My vital signs stopped by their hands, by yours,
which lower the ropes eight feet deep into the earth.
I can hear the dirt shoveled on top until there is no sound.
The weight warps the wood closer to my face.

You hated to be the one to do that to me, you said,
Like there had to be someone.
I should have dropped a penny into your executioner's hand.

I should have said, "I forgive you."
There's freedom in feeling that there's no choice, I assume,
Freedom from the screams you hear from eight feet below;
Freedom from the pilgrims buried when they were comatose,
Dug up decades later to find their skeletons clawing to get out.
This freedom, I guess, makes you capable of what you do:
You spread the cold spoon like cold cream all over my body.
You insert it deep inside me like you.
You erase my name, banish me from your house like a Montague.
My unborn children with O-shaped mouths press against your window.
I, their murderess mother, who love them so,
Stare blankly back, mummified, for all they know.
Yellow and red rain pours down on my boy and my girl,
Wets their clothes, beats their eyes shut
Against my extenuating scream, one note—
The rain, red and yellow, relentless in its waning
When you cross my hands across my chest,
When your fingers force my face into an expression of repose.
Perhaps you love me best now I've matched the dead,
Buried alive by your fear that I am.
Winter trees tarry against the winter sky like wet feathers.
And I, as resistant, cling to the debris,
To the edges of the sinking place you picture me in.

You visualize (wishfully?) a zombie
Who meanders through the same streets as you,
My silhouetted figure, the negative state of my positiveness,
Always with me, a dead twin.
With my lips zipped together, my tongue carved out,
I've become all eyes and you cannot bring yourself to look into them.
For if you did,
You would hear my scream as just breathing, and you know it.
You would witness without surprise the green decumbence of my exile.
You expect the odor of putrefying flesh
But discover instead my body whole and pink,
Loyal to your touch as you once did.
From the inverted mouth, returns the bottomless kiss
From my hidden sex, a Buddha's smile,
My body, the beautiful box you fetishize
As if inside me there were a box even more beautiful.

Stripped of our clothes we go beyond the flesh through the flesh,
To the swelling within us we refer to as our souls.

Our flesh, a rope bridge to this, where trains pass beneath
In the night, in the philharmonic heat.
Where the red moon, inches above our heads,
Will exclude us from its light, apheliotropically, in the end.
And this is why we in our aphasia
Must kiss and kiss and kiss, in an effort
To include ourselves in the red moon and suffocating kudzu's eternity;
Which, if granted, we could not bear, we admit.
But equally we cannot bear its alternative, so we kiss
Flagrantly, tearing our shirts open
And eating from the other's mouth the other's mouth.
So we kiss, just once, a reminder, a glove, an interleaf
Of our aloneness spent together, for now.
So we kiss, cat and mouse, until our saliva becomes a kind of elixir,
Kissing insistently, petulantly, apologetically, tangentially, automatically,
Profanely our necks, our breasts, our sexes, our hands,
Our fingers in each other's mouths, our eyelids,
Until we kiss as if writing a beginning and a middle and an end to us
In the dilating myopia of our kiss.

And in the very last box (if there is one), a symbol
Offered up like a sacrifice, a sliver of jade.

Jade, the gemstone of prophetic dreams
Raised upon velvet, a yellow star, a pigmentation, the perpetrator of sin.

Raised upon velvet, it rises again in symbolic ascent.
The cremation dust of resurrection, lost as it nears the unifying sky.
Lost and scattered like snow flurry
Across the treeless plain where animal totems roam or graze.

Who sent the yellow star swimming in my veins?
Who plucked it out like an eye and painted it so painfully yellow to begin with?

Who stigmatized the pigmentation of my skin?
Who soaked me in blackness, rain of red and yellow, every inch?
Who shamed the muscular backs of two men
Making love in the privacy of their bedroom?
Outside, the purling insults deflect from their torsos.
And though six yods whirl, a natural pedestal at their feet,
Like a purdah, a curtain must be drawn in public;
A purdah of lamé, like the backs of two women
Making love in the privacy of their bedroom.

White bread, white collar, white shoe, white noise, tennis whites, Snow White, white
tails, white boy, white sale, white teeth, lily white, hospital white, white night, white
linen, white horse, White House, deathly white, white cloud, white lie, white elephant,
white wedding, bone white, soft white, semen white, white wine, white rabbit, white
glove, white Christmas, white blood cells

I hang from hooks that pierce my chest,
From threads in a hole eight feet deep without food or water.
I hang as if on a vision quest,
A grizzly bear existing on its own fat like an oil lamp.
I hang until I gather the grotto around me as my coat,
The fur of my grizzly bear totem on earth.
And listen, floating within this black tank
To the rain, red and yellow, pummel the surface above.

It pours down on those buried alive in Hades.
On all the angels, "Ti bon ange," trapped in their jars,
Music convexed inside tiny silver balls.
Boxes within boxes within boxes within boxes. . . .
And in the very last box (if there is one), inside us:
There is no yellow star, only a virus of hatred.
There is no pigmentation, only ignominious discrimination.
There is no difference, only lynching, gassing, and burning,
Only the indifferent, contributing insidiously
Like the president of our country,
Only power thwarted and twisted as vegetation on Three Mile Island,
Only fear that spills, injections of interferon, upon the agnostic cemetery,
Only fallout that pulverizes the monolithic granite,
Only tears precipitating on the multicolored florets
That appear more as if tossed than placed, like wedding nosegays,
Before the engraved names and dates of the arbitrary lengths of life—
Only the atrophied hearts of the living that look on.

While I, in a kind of sunk ship of my own, listen
To the falling of our love, flayed in its attempt to be shown.
Until burying what was left of our desire
Was all that was left,
Box within box, into the cold slid the black body bag.
I can hear the wings around me beat against their jars,
The frenetic angels fighting for air.
Their letters, conversations, monologues of defenses, possessions, mementos,
Telephones, typewriters, telegrams, sexual innuendoes and actual gestures,
Assimilate a soliloquy that has become an abyss.

Abysmally falling on the flavescent grass,
Falling and simultaneously bursting inside me,
Box within box within box within box. . . .
Violently, sequentially, the boxes spring open their lids.

And in the very last box (if there is one), inside me,
Lies the root laid upon velvet,
Simply a symbol like a sliver of jade:
A cold spoon, an antibody, a yellow star, a pigmentation.
"What's Montague? It is not hand, nor foot, nor arm, nor face."
The mythology of white weaves these threads from which I hang.
Jade, the gemstone of prophetic dreams,
Dissolves in my system like a pill.
I watch vigilantly while you take off your surgical gloves,
I watch you approach and drink from my cup,
For I've put no pufferfish powder in there, you finally trust.
Finally my healthy body that is my healthy body is given back to me.
Finally my rights that are my rights, as my tongue is mine, are regained.
Finally you touch me, and the finality explodes
Into plains of thought, layers of earth in an archaeological site,
Into the history of boxes,
Until finally they collapse within themselves
And vanish into extinction.

Future Text Panel

A fire going is the only sound
of my old life shrinking on the left with the sun.

The treetops, prolific as the sky, hide the sky.

My blood unnerves me.

The evidence of friends exists only in memory,
as if they were dead, or as if I were dead,
my spirit slithering throughout the earth,
perhaps seeking revenge,
or in search of the deed I need to complete
to finally leave my body in peace
like a personage.

Bound to the unfinished,
silt still spills upon my grave,
upon my name engraved
I must wear in my exodus like Houdini's chains.

Poem for a Poem

for "Jade"

And the snow fell lightly in Cambridge
where I swallowed the lightning of you whole,
a bolt with such a hyperbolic zigzag to its edges
that it seemed cut out of cardboard for a school play.
It stayed that way, stuck inside me like a pipe,
a spine of bite-sized bones.
And the snow fell lightly in Cambridge
where I stood on the platform in public for you,
you placed precariously before me like sheet music,
just paper, I know,
but not outside of me as I had hoped,
and I wrote that winter in those black mornings.
And the snow fell lightly in Cambridge.
My lamp snowed whitely on my desk, a street of snow
where white mice multiply by the hundreds.
And everything was so cold, all my animate objects,
except for the lead of my pencil, a welding utensil
or flashlight to guide my exodus in the snow.
I wrote you, a wagon I pulled on the road
in the effort to leave you, to let you go.
Or maybe it was more the other way around,
the words, bread crumbs strewn to lead me back home.
Does it matter, really, which direction I desired?
I built, plank by plank, the rope bridge with so much purpose
that the purpose became the purpose in itself:
the relief of the labor of mindless work,
the stinging panic that brought lovely focus
to the next cliff. The next cliff
was all I thought about, as if sailing in a ship at dawn.
And the snow fell lightly in Cambridge.
So whitely it put me back in my days,
the hotel decor as monochromatic as my thoughts
of you, you the poem, and the you in the poem,
the two merging together like a photograph

when a matte finish snapshot is what I have left.
The landscape behind the amateur portrait
landscapes the landscape of my pain, rank with weeds
outlasting of you, or me, as landscapes do;
though as a landscape of snow you'll always loom
where the lamplight on my desk whitely snows.
I thought because you were so complete,
because you came out whole like a baby
or twelve-foot snake yanked from my gullet,
great sword of Excalibur ripped from its stone,
that at last you were separate from me as a landscape.
But deeper you sank instead, absorbed into my liver
like a bottle of vodka I'd consumed.
Now there's no getting rid of you.
I could tear you up, burn you, stubbornly disown you,
sign a pen name in place of my own,
and still you'd roll through my head, a motion picture,
sway below me still the sturdy net I wove of you that winter.
I even feel guilty and somewhat fearful
as if you had the power to paralyze my hands,
break every bone in my fingers like a king,
draw and quarter me for my traitorousness;
then turn all my poems to mush, as if they be, by the grace
of god, not already that.
And with the spiteful vengeance of a jilted lover
ensure supernaturally that they never be read,
for they're not made of the pure substance of you,
like the real thing I shot up my veins,
and let the much-talked-about bliss run rampant,
not caring, not caring about anything.
Ironically I wrote you to make myself clean,
a thousand baths taken in the writing of you,
the symbolic cleansing of a baptismal crucifix.
Now you riddle me permanently, bodily, a body tattoo,
internally ruinous, a virus and not just deadly
but deadening to all other poems and men.
Everything breaks down to the denomination of you,
everything I write simply the dissemination of you,
replicating in my body. O my molecule.

MELVIN DIXON

Melvin Dixon died of AIDS-related complications in 1992, when he was forty-two. He was the author of the novels Trouble the Waters *and* Vanishing Rooms; *a critical work,* Ride Out the Wilderness: Geography and Identity in African-American Literature; *and two collections of poems, including the posthumously published* Love's Instruments. *He also translated from the French* The Collected Poems of Leopold Sedar Senghor. *In "I'll Be Somewhere Listening for My Name," his closing address at OUTWRITE 92: The Third National Lesbian and Gay Writers Conference, he said: "I come to you bearing witness to a broken heart; I come to you bearing witness to a broken body—but a witness to an unbroken spirit. Perhaps it is only to you that such witness can be brought and its jagged edges softened a bit and made meaningful. . . . What kind of witness will you bear? What truthtelling are you brave enough to utter and endure the consequences of your unpopular message?"*

The Falling Sky

In Memory of Chester Weinerman

This lonely hour in autumn, this thick November sky,
Memory hovers above us like the threat of rain
Or razor blades of sun and shooting stars.
I could never catch a baseball, never throw one.
At bat or in the field, I'd chop madly and flail
My windmill arms at the air, at the air,
All under the jeering, brilliant laughter of the blue,
"Easy out. Easy out!"

When at last you knew the sky was falling
You were too sick to go outside, even when lightning
Broke the day into pieces shimmering down.
But in my dream you bolted from the bed.
You ran to us, screaming "Save me. Save me!"
And we held you tight, held onto your visible bones.

Now I, too, have started to thin and sweat and cough.
Once again the low clouds conspire, playground bullies
Their laughter bursting into gloom and gray.
Dust already gathers at the grit line of my teeth.
Ash coats my skin like a uniform with no number.
The wind whirls through the deserted diamond field,
And my hands scramble at the fast falling sky,
And a sudden, unknown voice cries out:
"Come on, catch it. You can do it. Catch it."

Blood Positive

1. *The Children Wonder*

What did you do when the thighs of our brothers
were nothing but bruises and bones?
Where did you go when the songs said to march
and you only meandered and minced?
Whom did you kiss with your cough
and elaborate phlegm? How much time
did you borrow on blood?
What was the price of your fear and your fist?

DON'T MOVE.

YOUR MEMORY OR YOUR LIFE.

2. *The Dead Speak*

Leave us alone.
We did nothing but worship our kind.
When you love as we did you will know
there is no life but this
and history will not be kind.
Now take what you need and get out.

Wednesday Mourning

Morning blood on my pillow,
dried brown from the night fighting me
and I don't know why.

I check myself and find no cuts,
no pimples scratched off, no teeth
loose and gummy, no fingers peeled,

but lips swollen from calling his name
and feeling my head and throat run dry—
the fluids fled are body tears
that take their mourning weight.

My head empties after drink or dream.
But this is not the first blood—two,
three, four mornings straight,
in different pillow spots when I awake

and coloring my whole day red.
My eyes tell it: someone
upstairs inside me is dying
not the first death.

TIM DLUGOS

Tim Dlugos was born in 1950 in East Longmeadow, Massachusetts, and grew up in suburban Washington, D.C., where he was associated with Mass Transit, a group of Washington-based poets that included Michael Lally and Terence Winch. In the mid-1970s he moved to New York, where he was a board member of The Poetry Project at St. Mark's Church-in-the-Bowery and a contributing editor of Christopher Street. *At the time of his death, from AIDS-related complications, in 1990, he was pursuing graduate studies at Yale Divinity School. His works include such chapbooks as* Je Suis Ein Amerikaner *and* Entre Nous, *and two full-length collections of poems,* Strong Place *and* Powerless, *both of which were published posthumously.*

G-9

I'm at a double wake
in Springfield, for a childhood
friend and his father
who died years ago. I join
my aunt in the queue of mourners
and walk into a brown study,
a sepia room with books
and magazines. The father's
in a coffin; he looks exhumed,
the worse for wear. But where
my friend's remains should be
there's just the empty base
of an urn. Where are his ashes?
His mother hands me
a paper cup with pills:
leucovorin, Zovirax,
and AZT. "Henry
wanted you to have these,"
she sneers. "Take all
you want, for all the good
they'll do." "Dlugos.
Meester Dlugos." A lamp
snaps on. Raquel,
not Welch, the chubby
nurse, is standing by my bed.
It's 6 a.m., time to flush
the heplock and hook up
the I.V. line. False dawn
is changing into day, infusing
the sky above the Hudson

with a flush of light.
My roommate stirs
beyond the pinstriped curtain.
My first time here on G-9,
the AIDS ward, the cheery
D & D Building intentionality
of the decor made me feel
like jumping out a window.
I'd been lying on a gurney
in an E.R. corridor
for nineteen hours, next to
a psychotic druggie
with a voice like Abbie
Hoffman's. He was tied
up, or down, with strips
of cloth (he'd tried to slug
a nurse) and sent up
a grating adenoidal whine
all night. "Nurse . . . nurse . . .
untie me, *please* . . . these
rags have strange powers."
By the time they found
a bed for me, I was in
no mood to appreciate the clever
curtains in my room,
the same fabric exactly
as the drapes and sheets
of a P-town guest house
in which I once—partied? stayed?
All I can remember is
the pattern. Nor did it
help to have the biggest queen
on the nursing staff
clap his hands delightedly
and welcome me to AIDS-land.
I wanted to drop
dead immediately. That
was the low point. Today
these people are my friends,
in the process of restoring
me to life a second time.
I can walk and talk
and breathe simultaneously

now. I draw a breath
and sing "Happy Birthday"
to my roommate Joe.
He's 51 today. I didn't think
he'd make it. Three weeks
ago they told him that he had
aplastic anemia, and nothing
could be done. Joe had been
a rotten patient, moaning
operatically, throwing chairs
at nurses. When he got
the bad news, there was
a big change. He called
the relatives with whom
he had been disaffected,
was anointed and communicated
for the first time since the age
of eight when he was raped
by a priest, and made a will.
As death drew nearer, Joe
grew nicer, almost serene.
Then the anemia
began to disappear, not
because of medicines, but
on its own. Ready to die,
it looks like Joe has more
of life to go. He'll go
home soon. "When will *you*
get out of here?" he asks me.
I don't know; when the X-ray
shows no more pneumonia.
I've been here three weeks
this time. What have I
accomplished? Read some
Balzac, spent "quality
time" with friends, come back
from death's door, and
prayed, prayed a lot.
Barry Bragg, a former
lover of a former
lover and a new
Episcopalian, has AIDS too,
and gave me a leatherbound

and gold-trimmed copy of the Office,
the one with all the antiphons.
My list of daily intercessions
is as long as a Russian
novel. I pray about AIDS
last. Last week I made a list
of all my friends who've died
or who are living and infected.
Every day since, I've remembered
someone I forgot to list.
This morning it was Chasen
Gaver, the performance poet
from DC. I don't know
if he's still around. I liked
him and could never stand
his poetry, which made it
difficult to be a friend,
although I wanted to defend
him one excruciating night
at a Folio reading, where
Chasen snapped his fingers
and danced around spouting
frothy nonsense about Andy
Warhol to the rolling eyes
of self-important "language-
centered" poets, whose dismissive
attitude and ugly manners
were worse by far than anything
that Chasen ever wrote.
Charles was his real name;
a classmate at Antioch
dubbed him "Chasen," after
the restaurant, I guess.
Once I start remembering,
so much comes back.
There are forty-nine names
on my list of the dead,
thirty-two names of the sick.
Cookie Mueller changed
lists Saturday. They all
will, I guess, the living,
I mean, unless I go
before them, in which case

I may be on somebody's
list myself. It's hard
to imagine so many people
I love dying, but no harder
than to comprehend so many
already gone. My beloved
Bobby, maniac and boyfriend.
Barry reminded me that he
had sex with Bobby
on the coat pile at his Christmas
party, two years in a row.
That's the way our life
together used to be, a lot
of great adventures. Who'll
remember Bobby's stories
about driving in his debutante
date's father's white Mercedes
from hole to hole of the golf course
at the poshest country club
in Birmingham at 3 a.m.,
or taking off his clothes
in the redneck bar on a dare,
or working on *Stay Hungry*
as the dresser of a then-
unknown named Schwarzenegger.
Who will be around to anthologize
his purple cracker similes:
"Sweatin' like a nigger
on Election Day," "Hotter
than a half-fucked fox
in a forest fire." The ones
that I remember have to do
with heat, Bobby shirtless,
sweating on the dance floor
of the tiny bar in what is now
a shelter for the indigent
with AIDS on the dockstrip,
stripping shirts off Chuck Shaw,
Barry Bragg and me, rolling
up the torn rags, using them
as pom-poms, then bolting
off down West Street, gracefully
(despite the overwhelming

weight of his inebriation)
vaulting over trash cans
as he sang, "I like to be
in America" in a Puerto Rican
accent. When I pass,
who'll remember, who will care
about these joys and wonders?
I'm haunted by that more
than by the faces
of the dead and dying.
A speaker crackles near
my bed and nurses
streak down the corridor.
The black guy on the respirator
next door bought the farm,
Maria tells me later, but
only when I ask. She has tears
in her eyes. She'd known him
since his first day on G-9
a long time ago. Will I also
become a fond, fondly regarded
regular, back for stays
the way retired retiring
widowers return to the hotel
in Nova Scotia or Provence
where they vacationed with
their wives? I expect so, although
that's down the road; today's
enough to fill my plate. A bell
rings, like the gong that marks
the start of a fight. It's 10
and Derek's here to make
the bed, Derek who at 16
saw Bob Marley's funeral
in the football stadium
in Kingston, hot tears
pouring down his face.
He sings as he folds
linens, "You can fool
some of the people some
of the time," dancing
a little softshoe as he works.
There's a reason he came in

just now; *Divorce Court*
drones on Joe's TV, and
Derek is hooked. I can't
believe the script is plausible
to him, Jamaican hipster
that he is, but he stands
transfixed by the parade
of faithless wives and screwed-up
husbands. The judge is testy;
so am I, unwilling
auditor of drivel. Phone
my friends to block it out:
David, Jane and Eileen. I missed
the bash for David's magazine
on Monday and Eileen's reading
last night. Jane says that
Marie-Christine flew off
to Marseilles where her mother
has cancer of the brain,
reminding me that AIDS
is just a tiny fragment
of life's pain. Eileen has
been thinking about Bobby, too,
the dinner that we threw
when he returned to New York
after getting sick. Pencil-thin,
disfigured by KS, he held forth
with as much kinetic charm
as ever. What we have
to cherish is not only
what we can recall of how
things were before the plague,
but how we each responded
once it started. People
have been great to me.
An avalanche of love
has come my way
since I got sick, and not
just moral support.
Jaime's on the board
of PEN's new fund
for AIDS; he's helping out.
Don Windham slipped a check

inside a note, and Brad
Gooch got me something
from the Howard Brookner Fund.
Who'd have thought when we
dressed up in ladies'
clothes for a night for a hoot
in Brad ("June Buntt") and
Howard ("Lili La Lean")'s suite
at the Chelsea that things
would have turned out this way:
Howard dead at 35, Chris Cox
("Kay Sera Sera")'s friend Bill
gone too, "Bernadette of Lourdes"
(guess who) with AIDS,
God knows how many positive.
Those 14th Street wigs and enormous
stingers and Martinis don't
provoke nostalgia for a time
when love and death were less
inextricably linked, but
for the stories we would tell
the morning after, best
when they involved our friends,
second-best, our heroes.
J. J. Mitchell was a master
of the genre. When he learned
he had AIDS, I told him
he should write them down.
His mind went first. I'll tell you
one of his best. J.J. was
Jerome Robbins' houseguest
at Bridgehampton. Every morning
they would have a contest
to see who could finish
the *Times* crossword first.
Robbins always won, until
a day when he was clearly
baffled. Grumbling, scratching
over letters, he finally
threw his pen down. "J. J.,
tell me what I'm doing wrong."
One clue was "Great 20th-c.
choreographer." The solution

was "Massine," but Robbins
had placed his own name
in the space. Every word
around it had been changed
to try to make the puzzle
work, except that answer.
At this point there'd be
a horsey laugh from J. J.
—"Isn't that *great*?"
he'd say through clenched
teeth ("Locust Valley lockjaw").
It was, and there were lots
more where that one came from,
only you can't get there anymore.
He's dropped into the maw
waiting for the G-9
denizens and for all flesh,
as silent as the hearts
that beat upon the beds
up here: the heart of the drop-
dead beautiful East Village
kid who came in yesterday,
Charles Frost's heart nine inches
from the spleen they're taking
out tomorrow, the heart of
the demented girl whose screams
roll down the hallways
late at night, hearts that long
for lovers, for reprieve,
for old lives, for another chance.
My heart, so calm most days,
sinks like a brick
to think of all that heartache.
I've been staying sane with
program tools, turning everything
over to God "as I understand
him." I don't understand him.
Thank God I read so much
Calvin last spring; the absolute
necessity of blind obedience
to a sometimes comforting,
sometimes repellent, always
incomprehensible Source

of light and life stayed
with me. God can seem
so foreign, a parent
from another country,
like my Dad and his own
father speaking Polish
in the kitchen. I wouldn't
trust a father or a God
too much like me, though.
That is why I pack up all
my cares and woes, and load them
on the conveyor belt, the speed
of which I can't control, like
Chaplin on the assembly line
in *Modern Times* or Lucy on TV.
I don't need to run
machines today. I'm standing
on a moving sidewalk
headed for the dark
or light, whatever's there.
Duncan Hannah visits, and
we talk of out-of-body
experiences. His was
amazing. Bingeing on vodka
in his dorm at Bard, he woke
to see a naked boy
in fetal posture on the floor.
Was it a corpse, a classmate,
a pickup from the blackout
of the previous night? Duncan
didn't know. He struggled
out of bed, walked over
to the youth, and touched
his shoulder. The boy turned;
it was Duncan himself.
My own experience was
milder, didn't make me flee
screaming from the room
as Duncan did. It happened
on a Tibetan meditation
weekend at the Cowley Fathers'
house in Cambridge.
Michael Koonsman led it,

healer whose enormous paws
directed energy. He touched
my spine to straighten up
my posture, and I gasped
at the rush. We were chanting
to Tara, goddess of compassion
and peace, in the basement chapel
late at night. I felt myself
drawn upward, not levitating
physically, but still somehow
above my body. A sense
of bliss surrounded me.
It lasted ten or fifteen
minutes. When I came down,
my forehead hurt. The spot
where the "third eye" appears
in Buddhist art felt
as though someone had pushed
a pencil through it.
The soreness lasted for a week.
Michael wasn't surprised.
He did a lot of work
with people with AIDS
in the epidemic's early days,
but when he started losing
weight and having trouble
with a cough, he was filled
with denial. By the time
he checked into St. Luke's,
he was in dreadful shape.
The respirator down his throat
squelched the contagious
enthusiasm of his voice,
but he could still spell out
what he wanted to say
on a plastic Ouija board
beside his bed. When
the doctor who came in
to tell him the results
of his bronchoscopy said,
"Father, I'm afraid I have
bad news," Michael grabbed
the board and spelled,

"The truth is always
Good News." After he died,
I had a dream in which
I was a student in a class
that he was posthumously
teaching. With mock annoyance
he exclaimed, "Oh, Tim!
I can't believe you really think
that AIDS is a disease!"
There's evidence in that
direction, I'll tell him
if the dream recurs: the shiny
hamburger-in-lucite look
of the big lesion on my face;
the smaller ones I daub
with makeup; the loss
of forty pounds in a year;
the fatigue that comes on
at the least convenient times.
The symptoms float like algae
on the surface of the grace
that buoys me up today.
Arthur comes in with
the Sacrament, and we have
to leave the room (Joe's
Italian family has arrived
for birthday cheer) to find
some quiet. Walk out
to the breezeway, where
it might as well be
August for the stifling
heat. On Amsterdam,
pedestrians and drivers are
oblivious to our small aerie,
as we peer through the grille
like cloistered nuns. Since
leaving G-9 the first time,
I always slow my car down
on this block, and stare up
at this window, to the unit
where my life was saved.
It's strange how quickly
hospitals feel foreign

when you leave, and how normal
their conventions seem as soon
as you check in. From below,
it's like checking out the windows
of the West Street Jail; hard
to imagine what goes on there,
even if you know firsthand.
The sun is going down as I
receive communion. I wish
the rite's familiar magic
didn't dull my gratitude
for this enormous gift.
I wish I had a closer personal
relationship with Christ,
which I know sounds corny
and alarming. Janet Campbell
gave me a remarkable ikon
the last time I was here;
Christ is in a chair, a throne,
and St. John the Divine,
an androgyne who looks a bit
like Janet, rests his head
upon the Savior's shoulder.
James Madden, priest of Cowley,
dead of cancer earlier
this year at 39, gave her
the image, telling her not to
be afraid to imitate St. John.
There may come a time when
I'm unable to respond with words,
or works, or gratitude to AIDS;
a time when my attitude
caves in, when I'm as weak
as the men who lie across
the dayroom couches hour
after hour, watching sitcoms,
drawing blanks. Maybe
my head will be shaved
and scarred from surgery;
maybe I'll be pencil-
thin and paler than
a ghost, pale as the vesper
light outside my window now.

It would be good to know
that I could close my eyes
and lean my head back
on his shoulder then,
as natural and trusting
as I'd be with a cherished
love. At this moment,
Chris walks in, Christopher
Earl Wiss of Kansas City
and New York, my lover,
my last lover, my first
healthy and enduring relationship
in sobriety, the man
with whom I choose
to share what I have
left of life and time.
This is the hardest
and happiest moment
of the day. G-9
is no place to affirm
a relationship. Two hours
in a chair beside my bed
after eight hours of work
night after night for weeks
. . . it's been a long haul,
and Chris gets tired.
Last week he exploded,
"I hate this, I hate your
being sick and having AIDS
and lying in a hospital
where I can only see you
with a visitor's pass. I hate
that this is going to
get worse." I hate it,
too. We kiss, embrace,
and Chris climbs into bed
beside me, to air-mattress
squeaks. Hold on. We hold on
to each other, to a hope
of how we'll be when I get out.
Let him hold on, please
don't let him lose his
willingness to stick with me,

to make love and to make
love work, to extend
the happiness we've shared.
Please don't let AIDS
make me a monster
or a burden is my prayer.
Too soon, Chris has to leave.
I walk him to the elevator
bank, then totter back
so Raquel can open my I.V.
again. It's not even
mid-evening, but I'm nodding
off. My life's so full, even
(especially?) when I'm here
on G-9. When it's time
to move on to the next step,
that will be a great adventure,
too. Helena Hughes, Tibetan
Buddhist, tells me that
there are three stages in death.
The first is white, like passing
through a thick but porous wall.
The second stage is red;
the third is black, and then
you're finished, ready
for the next event. I'm glad
she has a road map, but I don't
feel the need for one myself.
I've trust enough in all
that's happened in my life,
the unexpected love
and gentleness that rushes in
to fill the arid spaces
in my heart, the way the city
glow fills up the sky
above the river, making it
seem less than night. When
Joe O'Hare flew in last week,
he asked what were the best
times of my New York years;
I said "Today," and meant it.
I hope that death will lift me
by the hair like an angel

in a Hebrew myth, snatch me with
the strength of sleep's embrace,
and gently set me down
where I'm supposed to be,
in just the right place.

Parachute

The Bergman image of a game
of chess with Death,
though not in a dreamscape
black-and-white as melancholy
films clanking with symbols,
but in a garden in Provence
with goldfish in the fountain
and enormous palms whose topmost
fronds cut into the eternal
blue of sky above the Roman
ruins and the dusty streets
where any door may lead to life's
most perfect meal: that is what
I think of when I remember
I have AIDS. But when
I think of how AIDS kills
my friends, especially
the ones whose paths
through life have least
prepared them to resist
the monster, I think of
an insatiable and prowling beast
with razor teeth and a persistent
stink that sticks to every
living branch or flower
its rank fur brushes
as it stalks its prey.
I think of that disgusting
animal eating my beautiful friends,
innocent as baby deer. Dwight:
so delicate and vain, his spindly
arms and legs pinned down with needles,
pain of tubes and needles, his narrow
chest inflated by machine, his mind

lost in the seven-minute gap
between the respirator's failure
and the time the nurses noticed
something wrong. I wrapped
my limbs around that fragile body
for the first time seven years
ago, in a cheap hotel by the piers,
where every bit of his extravagant
wardrobe—snakeskin boots, skin-tight
pedal pushers in a leopard print,
aviator's scarves, and an electric-
green capacious leather jacket—
lay wrapped in a corner of
his room in a yellow parachute.
It's hard enough to find a parachute
in New York City, I remember thinking,
but finding one the right shade
of canary is the accomplishment
of the sort of citizen with whom
I wish to populate my life.
Dwight the dancer, Dwight the fashion
illustrator and the fashion plate,
Dwight the child, the borderline
transvestite, Dwight the frightened,
infuriating me because an anti-AZT
diatribe by some eccentric
in a rag convinced him not to take
the pills with which he might
still be alive, Dwight
on the runway, Dwight on the phone
suggesting we could still have sex
if we wore "raincoats," Dwight
screwing a girl from Massapequa
in the ladies' room at Danceteria
(he wore more makeup and had better
jewelry than she did), Dwight planning
the trip to London or Berlin where he
would be discovered and his life
transformed. Dwight erased,
evicted from his own young body.
Dwight dead. At Bellevue, I wrapped
my arms around his second skin
of gauze and scars and tubing,

brushed my hand against
his plats, and said goodbye.
I hope I'm not the one
who loosed the devouring animal
that massacred you, gentle boy.
You didn't have a clue
to how you might stave off
the beast. I feel so confident
most days that I can stay
alive, survive and thrive
with AIDS. But when I see
Dwight smile and hear his fey
delighted voice inside my head,
I know AIDS is no chess game
but a hunt, and there is no
way of escaping the bloody
horror of the kill, no way
to bail out, no bright
parachute beside my bed.

D.O.A.

"You knew who I was
when I walked in the door.
You thought that I was dead.
Well, I am dead. A man
can walk and talk and even
breathe and still be dead."
Edmond O'Brien is perspiring
and chewing up the scenery
in my favorite film noir,
D.O.A. I can't stop watching,
can't stop relating. When I walked down
Columbus to Endicott last night
to pick up Tor's new novel,
I felt the eyes of every
Puerto Rican teen, crackhead,
yuppie couple focus on my cane
and makeup. "You're dead,"
they seemed to say in chorus.
Somewhere in a dark bar
years ago, I picked up "luminous

poisoning." My eyes glowed
as I sipped my drink. After that,
there was no cure, no turning back.
I had to find out what was gnawing
at my gut. The hardest part's
not even the physical effects:
stumbling like a drunk (Edmond
O'Brien was one of Hollywood's
most active lushes) through
Forties sets, alternating sweats
and fevers, reptilian spots
on face and scalp. It's having
to say goodbye like the scene
where soundtrack violins go crazy
as O'Brien gives his last embrace
to his girlfriend-*cum*-Girl
Friday, Paula, played by Pamela
Britton. They're filmdom's least
likely lovers—the squat and jowly
alkie and the homely fundamentally
talentless actress who would hit
the height of her fame as the pillhead-
acting landlady on My *Favorite Martian*
fifteen years in the future. I don't have
fifteen years, and neither does Edmond
O'Brien. He has just enough time to tell
Paula how much he loves her, then
to drive off in a convertible
for the showdown with his killer.
I'd like to have a showdown too, if I
could figure out which pistol-packing
brilliantined and ruthless villain
in a hound's-tooth overcoat took
my life. Lust, addiction, being
in the wrong place at the wrong
time? That's not the whole
story. Absolute fidelity
to the truth of what I felt, open
to the moment, and in every case
a kind of love: all of the above
brought me to this tottering
self-conscious state—pneumonia,
emaciation, grisly cancer,

no future, heart of gold,
passionate engagement with a great
B film, a glorious summer
afternoon in which to pick up
the ripest plum tomatoes of the year
and prosciutto for the feast I'll cook
tonight for the man I love,
phone calls from my friends
and a walk to the park, ignoring
stares, to clear my head. A day
like any, like no other. Not so bad
for the dead.

MARK DOTY

Mark Doty is the author of Heaven's Coast: A Memoir and four books of poems, including Atlantis and My Alexandria, which won the National Poetry Series, the National Book Critics Circle Award, the Los Angeles Times Book Award, and the T.S. Eliot Prize. He lives in Provincetown, Massachusetts, and Salt Lake City, Utah. "I've written two books of poems and a prose memoir to try to begin to explore the impact which AIDS has had on my life and the lives around me," he writes. "I can't know, can't even imagine, who I would have been without this corrosive presence. I imagine that this must be true for gay men in America now generally: How can we think of ourselves apart from AIDS? What part of our experience, our psyches, hasn't it touched, darkened, changed?"

Grosse Fuge

This October morning,
soft lavender bursts above the Plymouth
parked on the neighbors' lawn: lilacs, wildly
off schedule, decking themselves a second time.
Downtown, on the Universalist green,
the chestnuts drop their sleek mahogany
under lanterned branches, tallowy blooms:
season of contradictions, tempest-wrought.
Summer's hurricane battered each branch bare,
skies suddenly wider, space in heaven
opened, our garden scoured as if by frost.
The little stars' jewel fires more consuming.
That was August, but all at once we wanted
to unpack sweaters, wrap ourselves in warm,
saturated tones: gems and harvest, moss.
But when real autumn came, the calendar
down to its last, late pages, the world
displayed its strange dependability
in disarray, rekindling: crocus
quickened, spiking through the fallen leaves,
then cherry and box-alder budded out,
and now this rash, breathtakingly sudden
bloom.
        Bobby arrives on a Saturday,
and sits on the end of the couch, scarlet
parka and a red Jamaican hat fished
from the closet pulled tight. Why's he so cold?
This false spring? No, he looks—how to say it?
—small, not just his circumstances but *him*

somehow reduced. His landlord doesn't want
him back, his sister's dropped him on the side
of the highway, at a rest stop, his clothes
in three flowered yellow pillowcases.
My mother, he says, *doesn't want me*
crying in the house, she doesn't want
my tears around. She fed him on paper plates,
kept his laundry separate and didn't tell
his father the diagnosis. We say
of course he can stay and Sunday he wakes
saying, *I have four things inside me:*
a backyard going around and around
in my head this way, lawn furniture
spinning the other way, and right here,
in my chest, chairs. It's not that they hurt,
it's that I can't figure how I'm going
to get them the fuck out. He never says just what
the fourth thing is.
                         This month the new comes
so dizzyingly quick it coexists
with all autumn's evidence: by the marsh,
the usual sumptuous russets, sparked
by pointillist asters. Rugosas dot
the goldenrods' velveteen. Tulips sprout,
the crab leafs out. How are we to read
this nameless season—renewal, promise,
confusion? Should we be glad or terrified
at how quickly things are replaced?
Never again the particulars
of that August garden: waving cosmos,
each form's crisp darkness in relief
against the stars. No way to *know* what's gone,
only the new flowerings, the brilliance
that candles after rain; every day
assuming its position in the huge
gorgeous hurry of budding and decline:
bloom against dry leaf, unreconciled sorts
of evidence.
                    I have been teaching myself
to listen to Beethoven, or trying to—
learning to *hear* the late quartets: how hard
it is, to apprehend something so large
in scale and yet so minutely detailed.

Like trying to familiarize yourself,
exactly, with the side of a mountain:
this birch, this rock-pool, this square mosaic
yard of tesserated leaves, autumnal,
a jewelled reliquary. Trying to see
each element of the mountain and then
through them, the whole, since music is only
given to us in time, each phrase parcelled
out, in time.
          Thursday he says *All night*
I had to make Elizabeth Taylor's
wedding cake. It was a huge cake,
with nine towers, all of them spurting
like fountains, and she didn't like it,
and I have to make it again, then
the thing was it wasn't really a cake
anymore.
          I am trying to understand
the *Grosse Fuge*, though I'm not sure what
it might mean to "understand" this stream
of theme and reiteration, statement
and return. What does it mean, chaos
gathered into a sudden bronze sweetness,
an October flourish, and then that moment
denied, turned acid, disassembling,
questioned, rephrased?
          MRI: charcoaled flowers,
soft smudges, the image that is Bobby,
or Bobby's head, or rather a specific
plane bisecting his head pictured on video,
cinematic, rich inky blacks, threaded
by filaments and clouds. I stand behind
the door, and watch the apparition
taking form beyond the silhouette
of the technician who wore gloves to touch him
(fully clothed, dry, harmless, but the coward
wrapped himself in latex charms anyway,
to ward off the black angel). On the screen,
like a game, he makes a Bobby of light,
numbers, and images—imagines?—Bobby
as atoms of hydrogen, magnetic,
aligned, so that radio waves transmitted
toward the body bounce back, broadcasting

this coal-smudged sketch: brain floating
on its thick stem, and little strokes of dark
everywhere, an image I can't read,
and wasn't supposed to see—but who could
stay away from the door? Which of these
darknesses, if any, is the one which
makes his bed swim all night with boxes,
insistent forms, repeated, rearranged?
In one of those, he says, *is the virus,
a box of AIDS. And if I open it . . .*

I bring home, from each walk to town, pockets
full of chestnuts, and fill a porcelain
bowl with their ruddy, seducing music
—something like cellos, something that banks deep
inside the body. The chestnuts seem lit
from within, almost as if by lamplight,
and burnished to warm leather, the color
of old harnesses . . .
                              *I have four bottles,
cut glass cologne bottles, right here, under
my ribs, by my heart. Can you tell the doctor?
I can't, he doesn't like me.*
                              Scribbled notes,
Opus 130: first movement: everything
rises to this sweetness, each previous note
placed now in context, completed, once
the new phrase blooms. Second movement: presto,
skittering summation of the first.
Next, andante broken open
by the force of feeling it contains,
tumbling out into moments of intense
punctuation, like blazing sumac,
goldenrod so densely interwoven
in the field I can't keep any of it
separate for long: pattern of cadence,
spilling out, forward, then cessations.
Like seeing, in jewelled precision,
exact, wet and startlingly *there,* oak leaves,
and birch, and exclamations of maple:
the flecked details of the piebald world.
Seeing it all, taking it in, and yet
rising up to see at once whole forests . . .

Is that it? All my work of listening,
and have I only learned that Beethoven
could see the forest *and* the trees?
                                    Bobby
cries on the couch: *All I want is one head.*
Later, *My head and my legs are one thing.*
Over breakfast: *Please, you've got to tell me*
the truth now, no matter what, swear.
The boxes, do they ever hold still?
They're driving me crazy with their dancing.
Mostly he looks away, mouth open,
as if studying something slightly above
and to the right of the world.
                                    The music
is like lying down in that light which gleams
out of chestnuts, the glow of oiled and rubbed
mahogany, of burled walnut, bird's-eye
maple polished into incandescence:
autumn's essence of brass and resin, bronze
and apples, the evanescent's brisk smoke.
But how is a quartet—abstract thing—
passionate, autumnal, fitful, gleaming,
regretful, hesitant, authoritative,
true? Is any listening an act
of translation, a shift of languages?
Even the music words themselves may make?
Flutter of pendant birch. Then I pull
myself back from the place where the music
has brought me; the music is not leaves,
music is not Bobby's illness; music,
itself, is always *structure:* redolent,
suggestive occasion, a sort of scaffold
which supports the branching of attention.

After the flood of detail the quartet
conjures, nothing: the great block of silence
which the fugue has defined around itself.
When I was seventeen, and everyone
I knew acquired a new vocabulary—*mantra,*
sutra, Upanishads—I learned a chant,
in Sanskrit, *gätē gätē pärägätē*
is all I can remember of the words
but the translation goes *gone gone beyond*

gone, altogether beyond gone, and that
is where the music has gone, and Bobby's
going,
            though not today, not yet. AZT's
a toxic, limited miracle, and
Bobby's in the kitchen, banging
the teakettle, cursing the oatmeal,
the first time he's been up in weeks. Last night,
when a Supremes song graced the radio,
he suddenly rose, coiffed in his blanket,
and lip-synched twenty seconds of blessed,
familiar drag routine. He's well enough
to be a bitch, to want a haircut
and a shave. Still too sick to go home,
—wherever that might be—and too ill, as well,
to stay: the truth is we can't live
in such radical proximity to his dying.
But not today. In the wet black yard,
October lilacs. Misplaced fever? False flowering,
into the absence the storm supplied?
Flower of the world's beautiful will
to fill, fill space, always to take up space,
hold a place for the possible? A little
flourish, a false spring? What can I do but echo
myself, vary and repeat? Where can the poem end?
What can you expect, in a world that blooms
and freezes all at once?
There is no resolution in the fugue.

One of the Rooming-Houses of Heaven

Last night I dreamed of Bobby again,
my old friend dead two years.
Funny that he's the one who comes
back to me; we weren't ever that close,

but sometimes I hear him talking
in the kitchen, while I'm cooking,
his disdain for whatever I'm dreaming up
almost affectionate. Last night

we were in a hotel between worlds,
the kind of place where he felt
most at home: good heat in the radiators,
easy rent, bath down the hall,

everything simple. We were lying around
on his narrow bed, something comfortable
about it, the green shade pulled
almost all the way down because

I wasn't supposed to see.
He was telling me—in his soft,
exasperated way, not too patient,
not too impressed with anything,

in confidence, as though possessed
of the best gossip—about the other world,
what it's like, though of course
I can't remember now a single thing he said.

Atlantis

1. *Faith*

   "I've been having these
awful dreams, each a little different,
though the core's the same—

we're walking in a field,
Wally and Arden and I, a stretch of grass
with a highway running beside it,

or a path in the woods that opens
onto a road. Everything's fine,
then the dog sprints ahead of us,

excited; we're calling but
he's racing down a scent and doesn't hear us,
and that's when he goes

onto the highway. I don't want to describe it.
Sometimes it's brutal and over,
and others he's struck and takes off

so we don't know where he is
or how bad. This wakes me
every night now, and I stay awake;

I'm afraid if I sleep I'll go back
into the dream. It's been six months,
almost exactly, since the doctor wrote

not even a real word
but an acronym, a vacant
four-letter cipher

that draws meanings into itself,
reconstitutes the world.
We tried to say it was just

a word; we tried to admit
it had power and thus to nullify it
by means of our acknowledgement.

I know the current wisdom:
bright hope, the power of wishing you're well.
He's just so tired, though nothing

shows in any tests, Nothing,
the doctor says, detectable;
the doctor doesn't hear what I do,

that trickling, steadily rising nothing
that makes him sleep all day,
vanish into fever's tranced afternoons,

and I swear sometimes
when I put my head to his chest
I can hear the virus humming

like a refrigerator.
Which is what makes me think
you can take your positive attitude

and go straight to hell.
We don't have a future,
we have a dog.
                    Who is he?

Soul without speech,
sheer, tireless faith,
he is that-which-goes-forward,

black muzzle, black paws
scouting what's ahead;
he is where we'll be hit first,

he's the part of us
that's going to get it.
I'm hardly awake on our morning walk

—always just me and Arden now—
and sometimes I am still
in the thrall of the dream,

which is why, when he took a step onto Commercial
before I'd looked both ways,
I screamed his name and grabbed his collar.

And there I was on my knees,
both arms around his neck
and nothing coming,

and when I looked into that bewildered face
I realized I didn't know what it was
I was shouting at,

I didn't know who I was trying to protect."

2. *Reprieve*

I woke in the night
and thought, *It was a dream,*

nothing has torn the future apart,
we have not lived years

in dread, it never happened,
I dreamed it all. And then

there was this sensation of terrific pressure
lifting, as if I were rising

in one of those old diving bells,
lightening, unburdening. I didn't know

how heavy my life had become—so much fear,
so little knowledge. It was like

being young again, but I undertood
how light I was, how without encumbrance.

And so I felt both young and awake,
which I never felt

when I *was* young. The curtains moved
—it was still summer, all the windows open—

and I thought, I can move that easily.
I thought my dream had lasted for years,

a decade, a dream can seem like that,
I thought *There's so much more time . . .*

And then of course the truth
came floating back to me.

You know how children
love to end stories they tell

by saying, It was all a dream? Years ago,
when I taught kids to write,

I used to tell them this ending spoiled things,
explaining and dismissing

what had come before. Now I know
how wise they were, to prefer

that gesture of closure,
their stories rounded not with a sleep

but a waking. What other gift
comes close to a reprieve?

This was the dream that Wally told me:
I was in the tunnel, he said,

and there really was a light at the end,
and a great being standing in the light.

His arms were full of people, men and women,
but his proportions were all just right—I mean

he was the size of you or me.
And the people said, Come with us,

we're going dancing. And they seemed so glad
to be going, and so glad to have me

join them, but I said,
I'm not ready yet. I didn't know what to do,

when he finished,
except hold the relentless

weight of him, I didn't know
what to say except, *It was a dream,*

nothing's wrong now,
it was only a dream.

3. Michael's Dream

Michael writes to tell me his dream:
I was helping Randy out of bed,
supporting him on one side
with another friend on the other,

and as we stood him up, he stepped out
of the body I was holding and became
a shining body, brilliant light
held in the form I first knew him in.

This is what I imagine will happen,
the spirit's release. Michael,
when we support our friends,
one of us on either side, our arms

under the man or woman's arms,
what is it we're holding? Vessel,
shadow, hurrying light? All those years
I made love to a man without thinking

how little his body had to do with me;
now, diminished, he's never been so plainly
himself—remote and unguarded,
an otherness I can't know

the first thing about. I said,
You need to drink more water
or you're going to turn into
an old dry leaf. And he said,

Maybe I want to be an old leaf.
In the dream Randy's leaping into
the future, and still here; Michael's holding him
and releasing at once. Just as Steve's

holding Jerry, though he's already gone,
Marie holding John, gone, Maggie holding
her John, gone, Carlos and Darren
holding another Michael, gone,

and I'm holding Wally, who's going.
Where isn't the question,
though we think it is;
we don't even know where the living are,

in this raddled and unraveling "here."
What is the body? Rain on a window,
a clear movement over whose gaze?
Husk, leaf, little boat of paper

and wood to mark the speed of the stream?
Randy and Jerry, Michael and Wally
and John: lucky we don't have to know
what something is in order to hold it.

4. *Atlantis*

I thought your illness a kind of solvent
dissolving the future a little at a time;

I didn't understand what's to come
was always just a glimmer

up ahead, veiled like the marsh
gone under its tidal sheet

of mildly rippling aluminum.
What these salt distances were

is also where they're going:
from blankly silvered span

toward specificity: the curve
of certain brave islands of grass,

temporary shoulder-wide rivers
where herons ply their twin trades

of study and desire. I've seen
two white emissaries rise

and unfold like heaven's linen, untouched,
enormous, a fluid exhalation. Early spring,

too cold yet for green, too early
for the tumble and wrack of last season

to be anything but promise,
but there in the air was white tulip,

marvel, triumph of all flowering, the soul
lifted up, if we could still believe

in the soul, after so much diminishment . . .
Breath, from the unpromising waters,

up, across the pond and the two lane highway,
pure purpose, over the dune,

gone. Tomorrow's unreadable
as this shining acreage;

the future's nothing
but this moment's gleaming rim.

Now the tide's begun
its clockwork turn, pouring,

in the day's hourglass,
toward the other side of the world,

and our dependable marsh reappears
—emptied of that starched and angular grace

that spirited the ether, lessened,
but here. And our ongoingness,

what there'll be of us? Look,
love, the lost world

rising from the waters again:
our continent, where it always was,

emerging from the half-light, unforgettable,
drenched, unchanged.

5. *Coastal*

Cold April and the neighbor girl
   —our plumber's daughter—
      comes up the wet street

from the harbor carrying,
   in a nest she's made
      of her pink parka,

a loon. *It's so sick*,
   she says when I ask.
      Foolish kid,

does she think she can keep
    this emissary of air?
        Is it trust or illness

that allows the head
    —sleek tulip—to bow
        on its bent stem

across her arm?
    Look at the steady,
        quiet eye. She is carrying

the bird back from indifference,
    from the coast
        of whatever rearrangement

the elements intend,
    and the loon allows her.
        She is going to call

the Center for Coastal Studies,
    and will swaddle the bird
        in her petal-bright coat

until they come.
    She cradles the wild form.
        Stubborn girl.

6. New Dog

Jimmy and Tony
can't keep Dino,
their cocker spaniel;
Tony's too sick,
the daily walks
more pressure
than pleasure,
one more obligation
that can't be met.

And though we already
have a dog, Wally

wants to adopt,
wants something small
and golden to sleep
next to him and
lick his face.
He's paralyzed now
from the waist down,

whatever's ruining him
moving upward, and
we don't know
how much longer
he'll be able to pet
a dog. How many men
want another attachment,
just as they're
leaving the world?

Wally sits up nights
and says, *I'd like
some lizards, a talking bird,
some fish. A little rat.*
So after I drive
to Jimmy and Tony's
in the Village and they
meet me at the door and say,
We can't go through with it,

we can't give up our dog,
I drive to the shelter
—just to look—and there
is Beau: bounding and
practically boundless,
one brass concatenation
of tongue and tail,
unmediated energy,
too big, wild,

perfect. He not only
licks Wally's face
but bathes every
irreplaceable inch
of his head, and though

Wally can no longer
feed himself he can lift
his hand, and bring it
to rest on the rough gilt

flanks when they are,
for a moment, still.
I have never seen a touch
so delibarate.
It isn't about grasping;
the hand itself seems
almost blurred now,
softened, though
tentative only

because so much will
must be summoned,
such attention brought
to the work—which is all
he is now, this gesture
toward the restless splendor,
the unruly, the golden,
the animal, the new.

DENISE DUHAMEL

Denise Duhamel was reared in Rhode Island and lives in New York City. Her books of poems include Kinky, Girl Soldier, The Woman with Two Vaginas, *and* Smile! *"I started publishing my poetry at about the same time as I became aware of AIDS," she writes, "so AIDS and its threat have been continually present, at least on some level, in my serious work. In 'David Lemieux,' I sought the sheer thump of repetition, as though repeating could mean some kind of answer or consolation."*

David Lemieux

My first boyfriend is dead of AIDS. The one
who bought me a terrarium with a cactus
I watered until it became soft. The one

who took me to his junior high school prom where I was shy
about dancing in public. The one who was mistaken
for a girl by a clerk when he wanted to try on a suit.

In seventh grade my first boyfriend and I looked a lot alike:
chubby arms, curly hair, our noses touching
when we tried our first kiss. My first boyfriend

was the only one who met my grandmother
before she died. Though, as a rule, she didn't like boys,
I think she liked my first boyfriend.

My first boyfriend and I sat in the back seat
of my mother's car, and on the ledge behind us
was a ceramic ballerina with a missing arm.

We were driving somewhere to have her repaired
or maybe to buy the right kind of glue.
My first boyfriend was rich and had horses

and airplanes he could fly by remote control.
My first boyfriend died on a mattress
thrown in the back of a pick-up

because the ambulance wouldn't come.
There was a garden in my first boyfriend's yard.
One day his mother said to us,

"Pick out some nice things for lunch."
My first boyfriend and I pulled at the carrot tops,
but all that came up were little orange balls

that looked like kumquats without the bumps.
My first boyfriend and I heard ripping through the soil
that sounded close to our scalps, like a hair brush

through tangles. We were the ones who pushed
the tiny carrots back down, hoping that they were able
to reconnect to the ground. We were the ones.

BEATRIX GATES

Most recently, Beatrix Gates is the editor of The Wild Good: Lesbian Photographs and Writings on Love. *She lives in Greenport, New York. "AIDS has been denied as a direct threat by many white lesbians," she writes, "and I have tried in the long poem 'Triptych' to show some of the daily consequences of AIDS, denied or alive, in our lives, in our homes, and on the street. In the poem reprinted here, the only resolution I have aimed for is to be sure every person pictured counts."*

Homeless

Section III from "Triptych"

Morning sun outside D'Agostino's, a young man bends,
crooked towards a parked car, heavy brown
raincoat, denim jeans and white shirt.
Smooth face, dark brown beard, hair shiny
in gentle curls away from his face.
His skin: translucent, taut across the bones
in his face, pink cheeks. His brow: a dome
over liquid brown eyes, deep-set under dark
eyebrows, long lashes. In one hand, he clasps
a sheaf of papers, his fingers curled.
He holds the papers up, shield at shoulder-height.
"Excuse me, I need help."
I walk towards him, he's not
threatening. I see his physical
weakness. "I was in a hotel," he says, "I was robbed,
they beat me up," I see the bruise on the side of his face
and look again into his eyes. I stop,
rest my bags at my feet. "It's dangerous
now," he continues, "it's no good anymore. They ruined it.
The addicts. They steal everything. They stole
my money, my medicine, my AZT. They sell it on the street."
His eyes start to brim, "I get my check this week, see,"
he holds the papers towards me, "see, here's my ID,
here're my papers. See, it's me." The tiny square
snapshot shows a large head, shorn.
I tell him to hold onto his
papers. I don't need to see
them. I ask if he's been to GMHC? "Yeah,
they got me a place, at the AIDS Hospice,"
he gestures down the street towards Christopher.
"GMHC only takes people under $5000, my checks put me over,

but they got me a referral to the hospice." He stops,
eyes brimming again, "I'm sorry," he looks down, shifts
his weight, stumbles in the space between the car
and the curb, touches my arm inadvertently, draws back
fast, "I didn't mean to touch you, I'm
sorry." "It's OK," I steady his elbow. "I'm so tired,"
he leans against the brown coupe outside the French restaurant.
"What do you need?" "I'm so ashamed, I hate asking
for anything. I ate out of a garbage can this morning.
I never did that before. I ate someone's leftover MacDonald's."
"It's OK, you were hungry, you got some food."
He begins to cry, then stops, "I'm gay, my father,
he's Italian, he's homophobic. He won't help me,
he disowned me, my father. He's so sick,
he doesn't understand, he's so sick, my father."
"What's your name?" I ask. "What do you need?"
"I'm so ashamed for asking like this,
I just have to. I got to get to the MacBurney Y,
they have a room for one night they said,
if I get up there. I need to rest. I have lesions,
on my legs," he pats his blue-jeaned thighs,
"they get infected, I got to clean them out, get
some peroxide." I know I have money
in my pocket, thirty dollars in the bank.
I reach in my pocket, pull out a ten
dollar bill, direct him, "Go out to Hudson, you know
the park . . ." "I need to sit down," he interrupts, "I'm so tired . . ."
"You know the benches, you can sit down and rest
or one of the benches down the street by the laundromat.
When you're ready, get a cab
on 8th Avenue. It'll take you right up
to the Y." I have never given anyone
a ten-dollar bill on the street before. "I can get your address
and pay you back, I get my check next week." "Forget it,
go sit down, go to the Y, sleep, rest." "I can't thank
you enough. Bless you, thank you," he crosses Greenwich
towards Hudson. I turn, my hands barely able to grasp
the two bags of groceries, lift the weight,
carry them around the corner.
I turn, see the back of his
raincoat, the beautiful chestnut curls
over his collar.

Next week, I am headed to the bank
to deposit a check. I am celebrating
inside, Thank God! Down to my last two dollars. Right outside
the bank, I see him at the corner of 8th
and West 12th in his raincoat talking
with a young woman clearly on her way to work.
She is gesturing, "Go to the Center, the Gay/Lesbian
Center on West 13th St," she is overpronouncing
her words. He is repeating, "the Center, the Center"
as if he has never heard of it. I pass them
quickly, fury carrying me into the bank,
Lying son of a bitch, goddam faggot, draining off women's
energy, lesbian energy like no one
ever dies from anything besides AIDS. Community,
my ass. How many faggots are nursing women
with breast cancer or anything else for that matter.
All he had to do was get to the fucking
YMCA. It didn't happen, goddam liar.
I make out my deposit slip, fill in
the date, bank account #, the deposit for $357,
sign my name. I decide to confront him
when I'm done, if he's still out there. *Remember me*
I'll say, *What happened to my*
ten dollars, you son of a bitch?
I pad quickly over to the express
deposit, put in my bank card,
check my balance: -$10.50. Shit, what happened?
I seal the envelope, pop it
in the slot, punch in the envelope number
and it drops safely in.
Get the deposit slip, $2 til tomorrow—$1
for milk, 65¢ for a cup in the morning, 35¢
for *Newsday*, and by 3 the check will be clear.
Minus $10.50, what happened?
Christ, who knows. At least I got
paid, I'll be OK.

Outside, the corner is empty, swept clear, a short
line to the ATM. *Remember me*
Maybe he wouldn't remember, maybe
he couldn't remember . . .
Why didn't he know The Center?
I begin to choke on my own breath

as I realize he may not remember.
AIDS in the last stages.
Is he lying or not remembering?
Is he dying or running a scam
or both? Does he know the difference? Do I?
Do I need or deserve to know
because I gave him $10, because
I'm a lesbian who has seen too
much of this disease?
Anything could have happened.
We live in New York City.
I wanted it to be simple: cross
the street, go sit down, rest,
get the cab uptown, then sleep.
In the morning breakfast,
take a cab to the AIDS
hospice. Here he enters the place where
he will die. I want to know
I have finished. But he has not
arrived anywhere. I bumped into him,
the motion of his life down the street.
He showed me that it was the world,
not he himself alone who held
his body in his hands.

THOM GUNN

Born in England in 1929, Thom Gunn came to the United States in 1954 and has lived for several decades in San Francisco. He is the author of numerous collections of poetry, including My Sad Captains, Jack Straw's Castle, Selected Poems: 1950–1975, The Man with Night Sweats, *and* Collected Poems. *"What did writing about AIDS tell me?" he asks. "Well, as far as possible not to write about myself, but to concentrate in my poetry on the man with AIDS— how he copes with it, how he dies of it. That is both more important and more interesting. Of course, I have written whiny poetry too, I'm human, but I've tried to do more of the other thing. Self-pity makes for seriously boring poetry, after all, and writing such poetry makes for a seriously contemptible human being."*

Lament

Your dying was a difficult enterprise.
First, petty things took up your energies,
The small but clustering duties of the sick,
Irritant as the cough's dry rhetoric.
Those hours of waiting for pills, shot, X-ray
Or test (while you read novels two a day)
Already with a kind of clumsy stealth
Distanced you from the habits of your health.

    In hope still, courteous still, but tired and thin,
You tried to stay the man that you had been,
Treating each symptom as a mere mishap
Without import. But then the spinal tap.
It brought a hard headache, and when night came
I heard you wake up from the same bad dream
Every half-hour with the same short cry
Of mild outrage, before immediately
Slipping into the nightmare once again
Empty of content but the drip of pain.
No respite followed: though the nightmare ceased,
Your cough grew thick and rich, its strength increased.
Four nights, and on the fifth we drove you down
To the Emergency Room. That frown, that frown:
I'd never seen such rage in you before
As when they wheeled you through the swinging door.
For you knew, rightly, they conveyed you from
Those normal pleasures of the sun's kingdom
The hedonistic body basks within
And takes for granted—summer on the skin,
Sleep without break, the moderate taste of tea

In a dry mouth. You had gone on from me
As if your body sought out martyrdom
In the far Canada of a hospital room.
Once there, you entered fully the distress
And long pale rigors of the wilderness.
A gust of morphine hid you. Back in sight
You breathed through a segmented tube, fat, white,
Jammed down your throat so that you could not speak.
How thin the distance made you. In your cheek
One day, appeared the true shape of your bone
No longer padded. Still your mind, alone,
Explored this emptying intermediate
State for what holds and rests were hidden in it.
You wrote us messages on a pad, amused
At one time that you had your nurse confused
Who, seeing you reconciled after four years
With your grey father, both of you in tears,
Asked if this was at last your 'special friend'
(The one you waited for until the end).
'She sings,' you wrote, 'a Philippine folk song
To wake me in the morning . . . It is long
And very pretty.' Grabbing at detail
To furnish this bare ledge toured by the gale,
On which you lay, bed restful as a knife,
You tried, tried hard, to make of it a life
Thick with the complicating circumstance
Your thoughts might fasten on. It had been chance
Always till now that had filled up the moment
With live specifics your hilarious comment
Discovered as it went along; and fed,
Laconic, quick, wherever it was led.
You improvised upon your own delight.
I think back to the scented summer night
We talked between our sleeping bags, below
A molten field of stars five years ago:
I was so tickled by your mind's light touch
I couldn't sleep, you made me laugh too much,
Though I was tired and begged you to leave off.

Now you were tired, and yet not tired enough
—Still hungry for the great world you were losing
Steadily in no season of your choosing—
And when at last the whole death was assured,

Drugs having failed, and when you had endured
Two weeks of an abominable constraint,
You faced it equably, without complaint,
Unwhimpering, but not at peace with it.
You'd lived as if your time was infinite:
You were not ready and not reconciled,
Feeling as uncompleted as a child
Till you had shown the world what you could do
In some ambitious role to be worked through,
A role your need for it had half-defined,
But never wholly, even in your mind.
You lacked the necessary ruthlessness,
The soaring meanness that pinpoints success.
We loved that lack of self-love, and your smile,
Rueful, at your own silliness.
                                    Meanwhile,
Your lungs collapsed, and the machine, unstrained,
Did all your breathing now. Nothing remained
But death by drowning on an inland sea
Of your own fluids, which it seemed could be
Kindly forestalled by drugs. Both could and would:
Nothing was said, everything understood,
At least by us. Your own concerns were not
Long-term, precisely, when they gave the shot
—You made local arrangements to the bed
And pulled a pillow round beside your head.

     And so you slept, and died, your skin gone grey,
Achieving your completeness, in a way.

Outdoors next day, I was dizzy from a sense
Of being ejected with some violence
From vigil in a white and distant spot
Where I was numb, into this garden plot
Too warm, too close, and not enough like pain.
I was delivered into time again
—The variations that I live among
Where your long body too used to belong
And where the still bush is minutely active.
You never thought your body was attractive,
Though others did, and yet you trusted it
And must have loved its fickleness a bit
Since it was yours and gave you what it could,
Till near the end it let you down for good,

Its blood hospitable to those guests who
Took over by betraying it into
The greatest of its inconsistencies
This difficult, tedious, painful enterprise.

Memory Unsettled

Your pain still hangs in air,
Sharp motes of it suspended;
The voice of your despair—
That also is not ended:

When near your death a friend
Asked you what he could do,
'Remember me,' you said.
We will remember you.

Once when you went to see
Another with a fever
In a like hospital bed,
With terrible hothouse cough
And terrible hothouse shiver
That soaked him and then dried him,
And you perceived that he
Had to be comforted,

You climbed in there beside him
And hugged him plain in view,
Though you were sick enough,
And had your own fears too.

The J Car

Last year I used to ride the J CHURCH Line,
Climbing between small yards recessed with vine
—Their ordered privacy, their plots of flowers
Like blameless lives we might imagine ours.
Most trees were cut back, but some brushed the car
Before it swung round to the street once more
On which I rolled out almost to the end,
To 29th Street, calling for my friend.
    He'd be there at the door, smiling but gaunt,

To set out for the German restaurant.
There, since his sight was tattered now, I would
First read the menu out. He liked the food
In which a sourness and dark richness meet
For conflict without taste of a defeat,
As in the Sauerbraten. What he ate
I hoped would help him to put on some weight,
But though the crusted pancakes might attract
They did so more as concept than in fact,
And I'd eat his dessert before we both
Rose from the neat arrangement of the cloth,
Where the connection between life and food
Had briefly seemed so obvious if so crude.
Our conversation circumspectly cheerful,
We had sat here like children good but fearful
Who think if they behave everything might
Still against likelihood come out all right.
    But it would not, and we could not stay here:
Finishing up the Optimator beer
I walked him home through the suburban cool
By dimming shape of church and Catholic school,
Only a few white teenagers about.
After the four blocks he would be tired out.
I'd leave him to the feverish sleep ahead,
Myself to ride through darkened yards instead
Back to my health. Of course I simplify.
Of course. It tears me still that he should die
As only an apprentice to his trade,
The ultimate engagements not yet made.
His gifts had been withdrawing one by one
Even before their usefulness was done:
This optic nerve would never be relit;
The other flickered, soon to be with it.
Unready, disappointed, unachieved,
He knew he would not write the much-conceived
Much-hoped-for work now, nor yet help create
A love he might in full reciprocate.

MARILYN HACKER

Marilyn Hacker's eight books of poems include Presentation Piece, *which was the 1974 Lamont Poetry Selection of the Academy of American Poets and a National Book Award winner;* Winter Numbers, *which received the Lenore Marshall Prize of the Academy of American Poets and* The Nation; *and* Selected Poems 1965–1990, *which received the 1995 Poets' Prize. Hacker, who divides her time between New York City and Paris, writes: "The face of AIDS I see through my life partner's daily rounds as a clinic-based care provider to HIV+ and AIDS patients in Harlem and East Harlem is largely dark-skinned, often a woman's, sometimes profoundly distrustful of the treatment options available, sometimes invested in quixotic hope. While my partner was still a mid-life student, I was myself diagnosed with breast cancer, which had, in the preceding years, killed several of our friends, including my partner's former lover, in early middle age. Two mortal diseases are striking down men and women in the prime of life, changing unalterably our perspectives on survival—and about our responsibilities to each other. The issues of AIDS and cancer have become inseparable in my own life and imagination."*

Against Elegies

for Catherine Arthur and Melvin Dixon

James has cancer. Catherine has cancer.
Melvin has AIDS.
Whom will I call, and get no answer?
My old friends, my new friends who are old,
or older, sixty, seventy, take pills
with meals or after dinner. Arthritis
scourges them. But irremediable night is
farther away from them; they seem to hold
it at bay better than the young-middle-aged
whom something, or another something, kills
before the chapter's finished, the play staged.
The curtains stay down when the light fades.

Morose, unanswerable, the list
of thirty- and forty-year-old suicides
(friends' lovers, friends' daughters) insists
in its lengthening: something's wrong.
The sixty-five-year-olds are splendid, vying
with each other in work hours and wit.
They bring their generosity along,
setting the tone, or not giving a shit.
How well, or how eccentrically, they dress!
Their anecdotes are to the point, or wide
enough to make room for discrepancies.
But their children are dying.

Natalie died by gas in Montpeyroux.
In San Francisco, Ralph died
of lung cancer, AIDS years later, Lew
wrote to me. Lew, who, at forty-five
expected to be dead of drink, who, ten
years on, wasn't, instead, survived
a gentle, bright, impatient younger man.
(Cliché: he falls in love with younger men.)
Natalie's father came, and Natalie,
as if she never had been there, was gone.
Michèle closed up their house (where she
was born). She shrouded every glass inside

—mirrors, photographs—with sheets, as Jews
do, though she's not a Jew.
James knows, he thinks, as much as he wants to.
He hasn't seen a doctor since November.
They made the diagnosis in July.
Catherine is back in radiotherapy.
Her schoolboy haircut, prematurely gray,
now frames a face aging with other numbers:
"stage two," "stage three" mean more than "fifty-one"
and mean, precisely, nothing, which is why
she stares at nothing: lawn chair, stone,
bird, leaf; brusquely turns off the news.

I hope they will be sixty in ten years
and know I used their names
as flares in a polluted atmosphere,
as private reasons where reason obtains
no quarter. Children in the streets
still die in grandfathers' good wars.
Pregnant women with AIDS, schoolgirls, crack whores,
die faster than men do, in more pain,
are more likely than men to die alone.
And our statistics, on the day I meet
the lump in my breast, you phone
the doctor to see if your test results came?

The earth-black woman in the bed beside
Lidia on the AIDS floor—deaf, and blind:
I want to know if, no, how, she died.
The husband, who'd stopped visiting, returned?

He brought the little boy, those nursery-
school smiles taped on the walls? She traced
her name on Lidia's face
when one of them needed something. She learned
some Braille that week. Most of the time, she slept.
Nobody knew the baby's HIV
status. Sleeping, awake, she wept.
And I left her name behind.

And Lidia, where's she
who got her act so clean
of rum and Salem Filters and cocaine
after her passing husband passed it on?
As soon as she knew
she phoned and told her mother she had AIDS
but no, she wouldn't come back to San Juan.
Sipping *café con leche* with dessert,
in a blue robe, thick hair in braids,
she beamed: her life was on the right
track, now. But the cysts hurt
too much to sleep through the night.

No one was promised a shapely life
ending in a tutelary vision.
No one was promised: if
you're a genuinely irreplaceable
grandmother or editor
you will not need to be replaced.
When I die, the death I face
will more than likely be illogical:
Alzheimer's or a milk truck: the absurd.
The Talmud teaches we become impure
when we die, profane dirt, once the word
that spoke this life in us has been withdrawn,

the letter taken from the envelope.
If we believe the letter will be read,
some curiosity, some hope
come with knowing that we die.
But this was another century
in which we made death humanly obscene:
Soweto El Salvador Kurdistan
Armenia Shatila Baghdad Hanoi

Auschwitz   Each one, unique as our lives are,
taints what's left with complicity,
makes everyone living a survivor
who will, or won't bear witness for the dead.

I can only bear witness for my own
dead and dying, whom I've often failed:
unanswered letters, unattempted phone
calls, against these fictions. A fiction winds
her watch in sunlight, cancer ticking bone
to shards. A fiction looks
at proofs of a too-hastily finished book
that may be published before he goes blind.
The old, who tell good stories, half expect
that what's written in their chromosomes
will come true, that history won't interject
a virus or a siren or a sealed

train to where age is irrelevant.
The old rebbetzin at Ravensbrück
died in the most wrong place, at the wrong time.
What do the young know different?
No partisans are waiting in the woods
to welcome them. Siblings who stayed home
count down doom. Revolution became
a dinner party in a fast-food chain,
a vendetta for an abscessed crime,
a hard-on market for consumer goods.
A living man reads a dead woman's book.
She wrote it; then, he knows, she was turned in.

For every partisan
there are a million gratuitous
deaths from hunger, all-American
mass murders, small wars,
the old diseases and the new.
Who dies well? The privilege
of asking doesn't have to do with age.
For most of us
no question what our deaths, our lives, mean.
At the end, Catherine will know what she knew,
and James will, and Melvin,
and I, in no one's stories, as we are.

Wednesday I.D. Clinic

For K.J.

Your words are ones the patients said themselves.
You carry them inside yourself, their vessel.

The widowed black man with two half-white children might
have given them up, have given up, this time

next month. But you don't say: that woman, this man.
You know their faces. You tell me a first name,

temperament and age, even a T-cell
count, if I ask, which will probably be less

than it was. Not always. Someone bursts into tears.
Someone drags his chair closer, to stare

at you, as if your eyes, your collar, your lips
said more than that sentence. He asks for vitamin pills.

She asks for condoms. He asks for simpler words.
She shifts the murmuring baby, lets him drowse

against her breast, bounces him on her knee,
starts, almost imperceptibly, to keen

a lullaby, or is it a lament?
As your heart beats, you rock her, in a mental

mutual embrace (you've hugged her) which allows
you to breathe with her, pause with her, swallow

the hard words. She's with you when you come downtown
later. You could keep it to yourself. You won't.

RICHARD HOWARD

Richard Howard was born in 1929 in Cleveland, Ohio, and studied at Columbia University and the Sorbonne. He is the author of ten books of poems, including Untitled Subjects, *which received the 1970 Pulitzer Prize in Poetry,* Two-Part Inventions, *and* Like Most Revelations; *he also translated from the French more than 150 works, including books by Gide, Cocteau, Camus, De Beauvoir, Breton, Robbe-Grillet, Barthes, and the complete* Les Fleurs du mal *of* Baudelaire, *for which he received the American Book Award. He is the poetry editor of* The Paris Review, *University Professor of English at the University of Houston, and a member of the American Academy and Institute of Arts and Letters.*

For Matthew Ward, 1951–90

who stipulated that I speak, at a memorial service,
of his "professional development," halted by AIDS

Out of the doorway, on a Soho street
where I had no reason for being (so I thought),
you stepped and stopped me, murmuring my name,
then yours, as if to rhyme—as if a tryst
had long since been agreed upon and drawn
        us both together
on an autumn evening, eleven years ago.
Together? I wonder. The lure was not to be
my Going Inclination of those years,
nor you the boy I greedily took you for—
as if the eagle had regained Olympus with
        the wrong Ganymede!
True, I would find you finicky to a fault—
you had been expertly tutored to serve Mass,
not empty ashtrays. Denver, Dublin, nuns
had worked their will, and by the time we met
your mind was a kind of sieve—the finer the mesh,
        the more it rejects!
Language, not love, was our only covenant;
no way to go unless it was This Way Out.
So together (at last!) we undertook a search
for the Just Word—translating, in your case,
being one more escape (that's what the verb
        means—*getting across*)
out of the frying pan into . . . an empty grate.
Eagerly, though, you began with Roland Barthes
whose *Fashion System* certified you had
a certain sour felicity of phrase,

and as far as I could tell—the interval
                was evanescent—
you had invented your living, if not your life . . .
Of course there were aggravations—perhaps the one
comfort I could give was this advice:
when Frenchmen talk, don't lift the needle off
the record, it will only go back by itself
                to the beginning.
And there *were* fulfillments. If you loved
the toils of such an enterprise
more than others love its low rewards,
you would be blessed by the paradox of form:
insides are always larger than outsides. Meursault
                in *your* voice sounded
much too good to be a good translation—
not the absence of thinking but its end;
in the scruple of *your* lexicon Colette
showed less anxiety about civilized things
than optimism about the savage ones:
                this you did not share,
yet showed it to be hers. You were, after all,
a friend to women and a lover of men.
Whereby came the horror, and a call
at midnight to announce, in tears, your doom.
Diagnosis loomed as the commonest disease,
                and you decided
to learn for yourself. You would make your life
your argument, decamping at thirty-nine
like Schweitzer for the darkest continent
and a hospital. You argued against your friends,
for sickness tries to shrink the world to itself,
                and we were what world
you had. No need, you told us from the first,
to be afraid of death—*you* wouldn't be there
when that occurred. The twenty friends who were,
watching you disappear before you died—
loss by daily loss—were quite afraid,
                and with good reason:
how could you forgive such presences
when you would soon be gone? Jesus said
Forgive our enemies—nothing about our friends . . .
Matthew, I speak unforgiven, having no wish
to commemorate you in your accomplishments,

> though forced to do so
by your dying writ. Our gifts belong to the world,
whether avowed or privately bestowed;
but our failings—all that we cannot give away—
belong to those who love us, those we love.
And though I come to praise your enterprise
> (which is mine as well),
I offer in parting no praise for your success,
nor pride in the promise of your career. I claim
no more than what, if you loved me, is my share
of your folly, your madness, your sickness and your death.
That is all I have of you and all
> a lover deserves.

"Man Who Beat Up Homosexuals Reported to Have AIDS Virus"

—*The New York Times*, March 8, 1991

to the memory of Allen Barnett

To *The New York Times:* Your health editor
may not print this; my social-worker says
> it will do me good
to write it anyway, and in my case
the terminal treatment has to be truth.
> Not much else, by now,
can "do me good": the hospital routine
laboriously contends with new bouts
> of pneumocystis,
thereby bestowing leisure to survey
my escalating KS lesions—caught
> *red-handed* . . . Last week
you ran an article about a man
whose name you withhold, though his age agrees
> with his appearance
when I was in his hands, and he in mine.
This was years ago, long before there was
> a reason to think
such handling was red, or led to being dead!
I can identify him all the same,
> though all different
from actions in which he says he took part.

—If he took part, then which of us took all?
    For all was taken,
as you report: I am one of the "many
gay men beaten in the 1980's
    by a truck-driver
in the New York area," and I owe
myself whatever account I can give
    of that episode.
It is not the reason I am here, nor
is my being here the result of it—
    but it represents
one dimension of the life I am in
a final position (no evasions!)
    to evaluate . . .

Maureen, it's Jane. Did you get the clipping? If you read it through, you realize why I had to call . . . No, now. We need to talk. You put things off, they just get right back on and ride you worse. It has to be Jack, Sis, your husband and the father of your girls! Everything fits. First of all about the life-insurance screening—what a way to learn he has that terrible disease! And then that part about "the large amounts of victims' blood on himself". . . Remember how hard it was—well, I can remember your complaining about it all the time—getting those stains out of his jeans each week! It was hard because that was blood—and not from lugging pork-bellies out of his truck! . . . I don't care what he told you, do you think I believe what Henry tells me? Of course you're not infected. How could you be if he hasn't . . . The paper said it's been ten years . . . Honey, I know: we're middle-aged, thank God! You don't imagine that Henry and I . . . ? Maureen, you've got to get it through your head there's something wrong with Jack. And I don't mean his getting sick now—wrong all the way back. Dumb of me to think the girls would tell you . . . Sis, do you understand how men get AIDS?

My social-worker says "we have to be
downright" (she invariably says
    "we" when she means me)
and goes on to assure me that *God is
in the details*—she doubtless heard the phrase
    in her Crisis-Class
("Depression and Dying") only last week.
It could be true, for all I know; there's not
    much hope of finding
Him in the Master Plan. So let's pray
she's right. Herewith the (divine) specifics:
    maybe five years back
I met Mr. X one Saturday night
—more likely it was a Sunday morning—

as I came around
the corner of Washington and Bethune:
a vision! He was playing with himself
    in the open cab
of a pork-butcher's van—such diversions
are often met with in the meat-market,
    appropriately,
since he asked, when I started cruising him,
if I wanted some. Meat. (I know you won't
    run any of this,
but I'm being downright.) So I went down
on him in the back of his truck. Dark there,
    hard to see—you have
to feel your way on such occasions—but
I found it easy enough to do that . . .
    I found it easy.

Why would he tell you . . . why tell anyone? A married man with three daughters: Maureen, he must have known people would never think . . . Did he ever think . . . ? And that would make it easy for him to do the thing he did—easier: he was their dad, whatever else he was . . . When did it start? Probably once you and he . . . stopped. Being in New York must have made a difference too. Because New York is different . . . from Nebraska, anyway. I'm not trying to be funny—you always said you hated living there, right up to when they transferred him back here . . . Maybe you knew why, even if there was no way for you to know . . . The paper said he went out looking for . . . the other kind (maybe they weren't so "other" after all) several times a week—you must have thought something even if you wanted not to. Maureen, the paper said "too many times to count"—no, "to remember." And it said the other drivers went out with him too. Does that sound right to you? Sis, when did Jack do things with others? Even beat up queers?

Once he was through, or I was—hard to tell
who it is completes such actions, who is
    active, as they say,
and who is passive (even a woman
is never really passive, I suppose)—
    once our thing was done,
he began talking to me in the dark—
till then, of course, he hadn't breathed a word,
    just breathed, and after
a while of breathing, the usual moan . . .
Maybe my downright talent made him feel
    he could shoot the works . . .
He asked, was that all I wanted to do,

and if it was, would I do something else
    for him. Something more.
He moved around, I knew what he wanted—
it was easy to tell by the clatter
    his belt-buckle made
against the floor. I started to explain
about my "proclivities" (not doing
    what my father did),
and as if, right then, something about *him*
had been exposed, something unbearably
    humiliating,
he began to yell and lash out at me
with that belt. If it was too dark for me
    to guess that my *not*
doing what he needed would enrage him,
it was also too dark for him to see
    where the hell I was:
I managed to slither out of *harm's way*
during the mayhem, and to haul myself
    eventually
out of the *van*, but not before we both
were something of a mess. That was my clue
    to my "assailant"—
there must have been blood, my blood, all over
the place, just as *The Times* reported it.
    All in a night's work.

He claims he hasn't done it in three years: maybe he doesn't need to do it now, but maybe he will. Maybe he has to. Maureen, you've got to trust your own sister: are there times when he takes it out on you? No one talks about beating, but I know it happens in a lot of "happy homes." I'm trying to help you. Listen to me! It could be years before Jack ever shows signs he has this thing—he may keep his strength for quite a while . . . I know you want to take care of him when he's not able to . . . when he needs help. It's a damn good thing you do—at this point I can't see why anyone else would: Maureen, he likes to hurt people! But you've got to take care of your-self first. If it passed into his blood from someone he beat up, what about yours? I suppose that's the only way it could happen now . . . Keep away from him if he—Sis, you know what I mean: if he can't go out for it, what's to keep him from beginning at home, like charity? I'm not joking, Maureen, I just want you to recognize the truth . . . If men are more devious than women it must be because they have more to hide.

But I doubt—being downright—if my man
had much to fear from me—certainly not
    from any of my

blood in any cuts of his, as he told
the Nebraska medical officers.
            I suspect—being
downright and outright—his dose could be traced
to an administration of the same
            bodily fluids
as those I was punished for declining
to provide. Not every faggot who climbs
            into a meat-truck
has my limitations, I know plenty
who would be pleased (*and* able) to oblige
            by humping a hunk . . .
Furthermore—being down and out—I couldn't
care less. I lie here wondering (most days,
            my only life-sign,
unless you count reading *The New York Times*
as a sign of life—and you would, although
            the *Living* section
is sometimes too much for me) . . . Wondering
is what my time is good for—good times! and
            what I wonder is
if the life I have always lived ("always"
being the last 20 years, who could know
            they would be the last?)
was mine at all, my choice—unless it was
just the life I could never acknowledge
            to *The New York Times*
(of course I'm using you as a symbol),
a life so sexually myopic
            I knew only those
faces I had kissed—and not always those!
Is this what it comes to? A tribal tale
            of A Thousand Nights
and a Night, except that this Scheherazade
gets herself 86'd . . . Sex turns out like
            reading (believe me
I know whereof I speak—in my corner
the comparison is anything but idle)
            because it gives you
somewhere to get to when you have to stay
where you are. But life is used up, if it's
            used, spent, or wasted . . .

Mama always used to tell us you get what you pay for. Maureen, that was a crock! I've learned better, and so have you, by now: you pay for what you get. Jack has to pay, so do you and the girls, Henry and I. The hard thing is to understand just what he got. Not Henry, Jack! Sis, don't be dumb . . . I know he got this disease, what I mean is, what did he get out of what he did that has to be paid for by getting AIDS? Damn right it's a judgment—isn't everything? I'm not saying he doesn't deserve it, it's just that if you're going to see him through to the end, you'd better understand the satisfaction—no, it's more than that: the rush, the thrill, or whatever it is doing things like that to other men could give him. If AIDS is so awful, then that has to have been so good. Do you see? You have to realize the joy of it if you're going to reckon up the pain. Think about it, Maureen. I'll call you back once Henry's gone to bed. We'll talk some more.

The *Times* keeps referring to a *life-style*
as having consequences. That is why
     I've made this gesture:
not to dispute your claim, but to insist
the consequences are *not* a judgment!
     This sickness I got
is no sentence passed on my wickedness—
recalling which "wickedness" makes up,
     now as before, most
of what I have lived for. Not died for,
I'm grateful, even to Mr. X . . .
     Why should his actions
incur a verdict, any more than mine?
By the time he reaches whatever wards
     Nebraska affords
(social-worker or not), I hope he can
summon up, as I did, the impulse that
     brought us together
and remembers me. That is what it comes
down to: a matter of remembering
     certain encounters,
certain moments entirely free of time.
I am no longer able to excite
     myself (is that verb
fit to print?), my visions are purely that,
just visions, endless reruns of the scenes
     I have collected.
Remembering is not even the word:
making comes closer. Where understanding
     fails, a word will come
to take its place. Making is my word,
my enterprise. Believe me, I lived through

     such episodes as
the sad one I have described for the sake
of . . . what? Of whatever was exchanged there
     in the dark meat-van
before the end . . . The second half of joy,
somebody said, is shorter than the first,
     and that gets it right.
Whatever's left of my life, I am *making*,
the way I made it happen all along
     —I replay the scenes
from that movie The Past, starring not
Mr. X playing opposite myself
     but Endymion,
Narcissus, Patroclus, all the fellows
I have welcomed to the tiny duchy
     of my bed—the world's
only country entirely covered by
its flag. I thank you for "covering"
     as well as you could
the story to which I have provided
such a lengthy follow-up—gay men do
     go in for length, or
at least go out for it; that is part of
our mythology. And now, perhaps, you
     know another part . . .
The nurse has just come in with another
delicious concoction. The social-worker
     awaits . . . (Name Withheld).

MARIE HOWE

Marie Howe lives in New York City and teaches at Sarah Lawrence College. She is the author of The Good Thief, *which was selected for the 1989 National Poetry Series, and the editor, with Michael Klein, of* In the Company of My Solitude: American Writing from the AIDS Pandemic. *She writes: "My brother John wrote letters that made me laugh out loud and cry so hard that I had to put the letter down; he also wrote and published some tender-hearted pornography under a pseudonym, and, the last year he was living, he sometimes talked about a serious piece he was working on—he called it* a b, a b. *He said he wanted to write something lyrical and truthful about everyday life, a kitchen table, a cup, a clean water glass. Sometime during the last six months of his life, he told me that* a b, a b *had developed into* a b c, a b c—*a third part had emerged. But he wouldn't read it to me. It was too early, he said, he'd read it when it was closer to being realized. After John died, I looked for it everywhere, among his small pile of personal papers, inside his desk drawers, under his bed. John's partner said he'd never heard John speak of such a thing. And I never found it."*

How Some of It Happened

My brother was afraid, all his life, of going blind, so deeply
that he would turn the dinner knives away from *looking at him*

he said, as they lay on the kitchen table.
He would throw a sweatshirt over those knobs that lock the car door

from the inside, and once, he dismantled a chandelier in the middle
of the night when everyone was sleeping.

We found the pile of sharp and shining crystals in the upstairs hall.
So you understand, it was terrible

when they clamped his one eye open and put the needle in through his cheek
and up and into his eye from underneath

and held it there for a full minute before they drew it slowly out,
once a week for many weeks. He learned to *lean into it*

to *settle down* he said, and still the eye went dead, ulcerated,
breaking up green in his head as the other eye, still blue

and wide open, looked and looked at the clock.

My brother promised me he wouldn't die after our father died. He shook
my hand on a train going home one Christmas and gave me five years

as clearly as he promised he'd be home for breakfast when I watched him
walk into that New York City autumn night. *By nine, I promise,*

and he was, he did come back. And five years later he gave me five years more.
So much for the brave pride of premonition,

the worry that won't let it happen.
You know, he said, *I always knew I would die young. And then I got sober*

and I thought, ok, I'm not. I'm going to see thirty and live to be an old man.
And now it turns out that I'm going to die.

Isn't that funny?
One day it happens: what you have feared all your life,

the unendurably specific, the exact thing. No matter what you say or do.
This is what my brother said: *Here, sit closer to the bed*

so I can see you.

For Three Days

For three days now I've been trying to think of another word for gratitude
because my brother could have died and didn't,

because for a week we stood in the intensive care unit trying not to imagine
how it would be then afterwards.

My youngest brother Andy said: *This is so weird. I don't know if I'll be*
talking with John today or buying a pair of pants for his funeral,

and I hated him for saying it because it was true and seemed to tilt it,
because I had been writing his elegy in my head during the seven hour drive there

and trying not to. Thinking meant not thinking. It meant imagining my brother
surrounded by light, like Schrodinger's Cat that would be dead if you looked

and might live if you didn't. And then it got better, and then it got worse.
And it's a story now. He came back.

And I did, by that time, imagine him dead. And I did begin to write the other story:
how the crowd in the stifling church snapped to a tearful attention,

how my brother lived again, for a few minutes, through me.
And although I know I couldn't help it, because fear has its own language

and its own story, because even grief provides a living remedy,
I can't help but think of that woman who said to him whom she considered her savior:

If thou hadst been here, my brother had not died, how she might have practiced
her speech, and how she too might have stood trembling,

unable to meet the eyes of the dear familiar figure that stumbled from the cave,
when the compassionate fist of God opened and crushed her with gratitude and shame.

A Certain Light

He had taken the right pills the night before.
We had counted them out

from the egg carton where they were numbered so there'd be no mistake.
He had taken the morphine and prednisone and amitriptyline

and florinef and vancomycin and halcion too quickly
and had thrown up in the bowl Joe brought to the bed—a thin string

of blue spit—then waited a few minutes, to calm himself,
before he took them all again. And had slept through the night

and the morning and was still sleeping at noon, or not sleeping.
He was breathing maybe twice a minute, and we couldn't wake him,

we couldn't wake him until we shook him hard calling, *John wake up now*
John wake up—Who is the president?

And he couldn't answer.
His doctor told us we'd have to keep him up for hours.

He was all bones and skin, no tissue to absorb the medicine.
He couldn't walk unless two people held him.

And we made him talk about the movies: *What was the best moment in*
On the Waterfront? *What was the music in* Gone with the Wind?

And for seven hours he answered, if only to please us, mumbling
I like the morphine, sinking, rising, sleeping, rousing,

then only in pain again. But wakened.
So wakened that late that night, in one of those still blue moments

that were a kind of paradise, he finally opened his eyes wide,
and the room filled with a certain light we thought we'd never see again.

Look at you two, he said. And we did.
And Joe said, *Look at you.*   And John said, *How do I look?*

And Joe said, *Handsome.*

The Promise

In the dream I had when he came back, not sick
but whole, and wearing his winter coat,

he looked at me as though he could not speak, as if
there were a law against it, a membrane he couldn't break.

His silence was the thing he could not
not do, like our breathing in this world, like our living,

as we do, in time.
And I told him: *I'm reading all this Buddhist stuff,*

and listen, we don't die when we die. Death is an event,
a threshold we pass through. We go on and on

and into light forever.
And he looked down and then back at me. It was the look we'd pass

across the kitchen table when Dad was drunk again and dangerous,
the level look that wants to tell you something

in a crowded room, something important, and can't.

What the Living Do

Johnny, the kitchen sink has been clogged for days, some utensil probably fell down there.
And the Drano won't work but smells dangerous, and the crusty dishes have piled up

waiting for the plumber I still haven't called. This is the everyday we spoke of.
It's winter again: the sky's a deep headstrong blue, and the sunlight pours through

the open living room windows because the heat's on too high in here and I can't turn
    it off.
For weeks now, driving, or dropping a bag of groceries in the street, the bag breaking,

I've been thinking: This is what the living do. And yesterday, hurrying along those
wobbly bricks in the Cambridge sidewalk, spilling my coffee down my wrist and sleeve,

I thought it again, and again later, when buying a hairbrush: This is it.
Parking. Slamming the car door shut in the cold. What you called *that yearning.*

What you finally gave up. We want the spring to come and the winter to pass. We want
whoever to call or not to call, a letter, a kiss—we want more and more and then more
    of it.

But there are moments, walking, when I catch a glimpse of myself in the window glass,
say the window of the corner video store, and I'm gripped by a cherishing so deep

for my own blowing hair, chapped face and unbuttoned coat that I'm speechless:
I am living. I remember you.

LYNDA HULL

Lynda Hull was born in 1954, in Newark, New Jersey; she died in 1994 in an automobile accident, while traveling between Boston and Provincetown, Massachusetts. In addition to her posthumously published collection of poems, The Only World, *she was the author of* Star Ledger, *which won the 1990 Edwin Ford Piper Poetry Award, and* Ghost Money, *which won the 1986 Juniper Prize. In his afterword to* The Only World, *Mark Doty wrote: "The pain of the last years of Lynda's life was, for her, a source of connection to the suffering of her times. Our century's great accumulating losses seemed continuous; from the Holocaust to the burning of Newark to the epidemic, what was erased was her family, her context. The poems track the terrifying passage of having seen it all, remembered everything, turned from nothing . . . She was a 'fortunate traveler' in that she was not numbed, not lost to any of those forces, external or internal, which would silence her. One response to horror—in Poland or Newark or Provincetown— is silence. Another is to make what one can, to create with all the more ardor and fury."*

Suite for Emily

1. The Letter

Everywhere the windows give up nothing
but frost's intricate veined foliage.
Just engines shrilling pocked and frozen streets
wailing towards some new disaster.
No *bright* angel's ladders going to split
heaven this Chicago instant where the pier's
an iced fantastic: spiked, the glacial floes
seize it greedy like a careless treasure—

marquise diamonds, these round clear globes, the psychic's
crystal world spinning in her corner shop
when I passed, a globe boundaried with turning
silent winds and demons. Out here the pavement's
a slick graffittied strip: *There's more to life
than violence.* Someone's added *Yes, Sex and Drugs.*
Hello, Plague Angel. I just heard your wings
hiss off the letter on my table—Emily's

in prison again, her child's lost to the State,
Massachusetts. Fatigue, pneumonia,
the wasting away. In the secret hungering,
the emptiness when we were young would come
the drug's good sweep like nothing else,
godly almost the way we'd float immune
& couldn't nothing touch us, nothing.
Somehow I'd thought you'd pass her over—

positive yes—but never really sick,
that flayed above her door there'd be some sign
of mercy. But there's only January's
rough ministry peeling my face away.
Light like the cruel light of another century
& I'm thinking of Dickinson's letter
"Many who were in their bloom have gone
to their last account and the mourners go about

the streets." The primer pages yellowing
on her shelf beneath an album of pressed gentian:
"Do most people live to be old? No, one half die
before they are eight years old. But one in four lives
to see twenty-one." She'd known the bitter sponge
pressed to the fevered forehead, the Death Angel's
dark familiar company, how she'd swirl her veils,
how she'd lean over the ewer and basin

blackening the water. This artic water, this
seething rustle—lamé, sequins, a glitter wrap
trailing from a girl's shoulders so the shadow pimps
go *hey princess, why you so sad tonight,*
let me make you happy, when she's only tired,
up all night & needing a hit to let her sleep.
We know that story, the crest and billow
and foam and fleeting fullness

before the disappearing. Discs of hissing ice,
doors you (I?) might fall through to the underworld
of bars & bus stations, private rooms of
dancing girls numb-sick & cursing the wilderness
of men's round blank faces. Spinning demons.
Round spoon of powder hissing over the flame.
Worlds within worlds, beneath worlds, worlds that flare
and consume so they become the only world.

2. Holy City, City of Night

What is that general rule which tells
        how long a thing will live? The primer answers,
Whatever grows quick decays quick: soon ripe,
        soon rotten. The rust-blown calla gracing
my table, those Boston girls 20 years gone,

young men in lace & glitter washed alien
    by gasoline sunsets, the burning sphere
lapsing below night's black rim. *Live fast, die* . . .

we know the rest. Reckless anthem.
    The pier cable's ice-sleeved beneath
my hands—miraculous, yes, to be here
    januaried by this lake's barbaric winterscape
Dickinson might read as savage text
& emblem of a deity indifferent. Her embassy lay
    beyond the city of jasper & gold, the beaten
wrought towers scripture promised the saved

would enter. What heaven she found she made.
    And so did we, worlds that sear, consume—earthly,
delirious. *Ignis fatuus*. Strike the match,
    the fizzing cap. But Oh Reader, the wild beauty
of it, the whirring rush, blonde hiss of aerial
miles, worn stairways in every burning school
    of nodding classrooms, the buzz-snap of
talk blurring hallucinatory fraught

avenues. Illusive inner city, drugged
    majestic residence spiralled with staircases,
balustrades rococoed, lapidary. Invisible empires
    dreamt beneath the witchery of birds
circling the Commons with twilight, their caw
& settle, the patterns as they wheel
    over the pond's reflective mirror bruised
roseate, violet, deeper, the swanboats

darkening into night's charged dazzle,
    Park Square joints gone radiant, the bus station
burnished before the zap, the charge the edge.
    It was the life wasn't it? Compatriots you'd
just love to die for, who'd jump you
in a New York minute. But the glory
    as the lights went up, torching the air chartreuse,
lipsticked pink, casting embers, seraphic fires

fallen earthward. Fallen, the furious emblems.
    We were so young we'd spend & spend
ourselves as if there'd be no reckoning, then grew
    past caring. All the darkening chapters.
Dream time, the inner time
where towers and battlements erect
    their corruscating glamour & how we'd glide,
celebrities among them, the crowds falling back,

dream deeper, gone & wake to day light's assault
    knocking another bare room, the alley, the bathroom
you inhabit like the thief you are. *Ignis fatuus*.
    I can follow you there, Emily, we girls
setting out a thousand ruined nights in the splendor
of the torched & reckless hour.
    Who wouldn't trade heaven for that fleet city
when winter beaks the shattered pane,

when summer's a nauseous shimmer
    of sexual heat, though sex is a numb machine
you float above. When the place you walk into
    is a scream in the shape of yourself.
When it makes perfect sense to blow someone away
for 20 bucks beyond even your bleak human universe.
    When the only laughter that falls down
is iron & godless. Here, I—the one who left—

must falter where persists
    this chrome traffic shrill, where the cable's
bitter alloy comes away in my hand,
    this metalled pungence of hair and skin
in wind persists riven as the taste of myself,
the blood blooming healthy
    real in my mouth, a future's lavish venues
spread stunned before me. These hands.

3. Combat Zone / War Stories

The district's been demolished, sown with salt.
The dazzling girls, girls, girls in platinum wigs
have been lifted away by some infernal agency,
the queens, exotic Amazons & rough-trade gay boys.

Sometimes I go back to walk the streets all shops
and swank hotels, the office blocks & occasional
burnt out shell. So American, this destruction
& renewal, cities amnesiac where evening's

genesis falls through vast deserted silences,
towers grown otherworldly with light
thrown starlike from some alien world. Gone the Show Bar,
the Mousetrap, the whole gaudy necklace

of lacquer-dark underground lounges, halls
of mirrors, music billowing dancers
clean out of themselves beyond the dead-faced tricks,
the sick voyeurs. The Combat Zone. I can map it

in my mind, some parallel world, the ghost city
beneath the city. Parallel lives, the ones
I didn't choose, the one that kept her.
In all that dangerous cobalt luster

where was safety? home? when we were delirium
on rooftops, the sudden thrill of wind dervishing
cellophane, the shredded cigarettes. We were
the dust the Haitians spit on to commemorate

the dead, the click & slurried fall of beads
across a doorway. In the torn & watered silk
of night, the Zone exploded its shoddy neon orchid
to swallow us in the scent of fear, emergency,

that oily street perfume & weeping brick.
Gossamer clothes, summertime and leaning
against the long dusty cars, cruising siren songs.
Summer? My memory flutters—had I—was there summer?

Dancer, and floor, and cadence
quite gathered away, and I a phantom, to you
a phantom, rehearse the story.
And now it's autumn turning hard to winter,

Thanksgiving, 1990, & all she wants is sweets
so it's apple pie barehanded & Emily's
spinning war stories, how bad she is: *So, I say,*
go ahead and shoot me, put me out of my misery.

Cut me motherfucker—my blood's gonna kill you.
Then she's too tired to sit & in the blue
kaleidoscopic tv shift I stroke
her hair, the ruined hands. *I didn't know*

how sick I was—if the heroin wanted the AIDS,
or the disease wanted the heroin. She asks me
to line up her collection of matchbox houses
so we can make a street, so we can make a neighborhood.

4. Jail, Flames—Jersey 1971

The psychic's globe whirls its winds: demons,
    countless futures, the pasts. Only
        thirteen the first time
    I saw you in jail, just a kid looking
up at me, the usual grey detective clamor,

inkpads & sodium flash. Hauled out by the officials,
    exemplary bad-news girl, they shoved
        a lyric sheet at me. Command
    recitation to sway you from straying.
"King Heroin," James Brown pompadoured like nobody's

business & here's Death cartoonishly aloft on a white
    winged horse, grim reaper lording it
        over the shivering denizens
    of a city, exaggerated as any Holy City,
going down, down, down. Just a kid, you, peering out

the jungle of your dark hair, greasy jeans a tangle
    of beads at your throat. Ludicrous,
        I know, me declaiming within
    the jail gleam that never sleeps all over us,
that effluvium of backed up plumbing. On my palm,

the bar's iron taint lingered for hours after.
    It didn't mean that much to me, 17,
        my practiced sang-froid
chilling the terror, that long drop
inside, the way you collapse to fall in flames.

I might have said you'll pay for the wild & reckless hour,
    pay in the currency of sweat and shiver,
        the future squandered, the course
    of years reconfigured, relinquishment so
complete it's more utter than any falling in love. Falling

instead in flames, burning tiles spiralling to litter
    the courtyards of countless places that will
        never be yours, the fingerprints,
    tossed gloves & glittering costumes, flared
cornices & parapets, shattering panes, smoked out

or streaked with embers, the tinder of spools, such
    a savage conflagration, stupid edge-game,
        the way junkies tempt death,
    over & over again, toy with it. I might have
told you that. Everything you ever meant to be, *pfft*,

out the window in sulfured match-light, slow tinder
    & strike, possession purely ardent as worship
        & the scream working its way out
    of your bones, demolition of wall & strut
within until you're stark animal need. That *is*

love, isn't it? Everything you meant to be falls
    away so you dwell within a perfect
        singularity, a kind of saint.
    Pearl of great price. Majestic, searing,
the crystal globe spins futures unimaginable, that

crucible you know so well, Emily, viral fever refining
    you to some essence of pain more furious
        than these winter trees
    stripped to black nerves above
the El's streaked girders, a harsh equation, some

god's iron laughter combing down time's blind
    & hush. *Hush child, forgive me.*
        Twenty years later, you say
    that night in jail you looked up
at me & wanted to be me. And I didn't care.

5. *Address*

Hello Death Angel, old familiar, old nemesis.
        In the deepest hours, I have recognized
your floating shape. I've seen your breath
        seduce the torn curtain
masking the empty window, have crouched with you
        in the doorway, curled in the alley
hooded in your essence & shadow, have
        been left blue, heart-stopped
for yours, for yours. Death,
        you are the bead in the raptor's eye,
Death you dwell in the funneling depths
        of the heavens beyond each
star's keening shrill, Death you are the potion
        that fills the vial, the night
the monuments have swallowed. You live
        in the maimed child wrapped in a wreckage
of headlines. Death you center
        in the fanged oval
of the prison dog's howl. Death you dwell within
        the necropolis we wake to in nightmare's
hot electric wind. You glint
        the edge of the boy's razor,
patient in the blasted stairwell. Everywhere
        you walk deep lawns, tvs pollinating air
with animals wired up to dance
        for their food, with executions
& quiz shows. You're in the column
        of subway wind roaring before each
train's arrival. I've seen you drape thoughtlessly
        a woman's hair over her face
as the shot carried her forward into stop-time
        & beyond anything she'd lain
her money down for. Death your sliver works
        swiftly through the bloodstream.
Hello Death Angel, Plague is your sister.
        I've seen her handiwork, heard
the tortured breath, watched her loosen the hands
        of the dazzling boys one from each other.
For love, love. I've seen the AIDS hotels
        & sick ones begging homeless
in the tunnels, the whispered conspiracies.

Shameless emissaries with your powders
& wands, your lunar carnivorous flowers.
   Tricks, legerdemain. I've seen you draw
veined wings over the faces of sleepers,
   the abandoned, the black feather that sweeps
so tenderly. I've seen the stain you scribe
   on the pavement, the glossy canopy of leaves
you weave. I've seen waste & ruin, know
   your kingdom for delirium, the furious thumbprints
you've scored on the flesh of those you choose.
   I've seen you slow-dance in a velvet mask, dip
& swirl across dissolving parquet.
   I've seen you swing open the iron gate—
a garden spired in valerian, skullcap, blue vervain.
   Seen you stir the neat halfmoons, fingernails
left absently in a glazed dish.
   Felons, I've cursed you in your greed, have spat
& wept then acquiesced in your wake. Without rue
   or pity, you have marked the lintels & blackened
the water. Your guises multiply, bewildering
   as the firmament's careless jewelry.
Death I have welcomed you to the rooms
   where Plague has lain when the struggle is passed
& lit the candles and blessed the ash.
   Death you have taken my friends & dwell
with my friends. You are the human wage.
   Death I am tired of you.

6. Dartmouth Women's Prison, 1992

Emily, delirium's your province.
You dwell feverish in prison
voiceless to plead
your need before the agencies
of government who *cannot hear the buildings*
falling & oil exploding, only people walking
& talking, cannon soft as velvet from parishes
that do not know you are burning up,
that seasons have rippled
like a beast the grasses beyond
the prison.

They cannot hear the strummed harp
of the nerves, black trees swaying winter,
cannot know your child is lost to you.

The human wage that's paid & paid?

Once, we were two girls
setting out towards that city
of endless searing night, the route taking on
the intricacy, the fumes & bafflements
of a life a woman might dream turning
feverish in her prison bunk. Probation violation,
when broke & sick, no way home
from the clinic the detective going
*ride with me, just talk, that's all
I want.* Twenty bucks and him crowing
we just love to run you little sluts in.

Em, if I could reach you through the dust motes'
spinning, infernoed dreams, I would dwell
in the moon's cool glistering
your cell, the rough cloth, the reflection
of your face given back in the steel basin's
water, in the smooth moan of women loving women,
a cacophony of needs. I am there with you lost
in the chaos of numbers, that nattering p.a. buzz,
in the guards' trolling clank & threat echoing
walls so eloquent
with all the high-frequency sizzle
of anguish they've absorbed.
Emily, I will bless your child, will
hold for you the bitter sponge,
would give you staff & orb, a firmament
radiant & free.

But these are phantoms, lies—
I cannot follow where you are. On my street,
the psychic's crystal globe whirls pasts, futures
but where you are is timeless.
*Pain—has an Element of Blank—It cannot recollect
when it Began—or if there were
a time when it was not—
It has no Future—but itself . . .*

Off the lake a toothed wind keens
& it's just me here, the one who's left.
Just me helpless to change anything caught
in this ellipsis between traffic, this
fleet human delay, all around
the wind singing like a mechanical ballerina
a girl might hold in her hand, the one
that watched your childhood bed, porcelain
upturned gaze, stiff tutu, dust in the folds
of that spindly piercing music sounding
of voices winged over water, becoming
water, & gone.

7. A Style of Prayer

There is a prayer that goes Lord I am powerless
 over these carnivorous streets, the fabulous
  breakage, the world's ceaseless *perpetuum mobile*,

like some renaissance design, lovely & useless
 to harness the forces of weather, the planet's
  dizzy spin, this plague. A prayer that asks

where in the hour's dark moil is mercy?
 Ain't no ladders tumbling down from heaven
  for what heaven we had we made. An embassy

of ashes & dust. Where was safety? Home?
 Is this love, staff, orb & firmament?
  Parallel worlds, worlds within worlds—chutes

& trapdoors in the mind. Sisters & brothers,
 the same thing's going down all over town, town
  after town. There is a prayer that goes Lord,

we are responsible. Harrow us through the waves,
 the runnels & lace that pound, comb, reduce us so
  we may be vessels for these stories.

Oh, the dazzling men torn one from the other,
 these women taken, these motherless children.
  Perhaps there's no one to fashion such new grace,

the world hurtling its blind proposition
    through space & prayer's merely a style of waiting
        beyond *the Hour of Lead*—

Remembered, if outlived,
    As Freezing persons, recollect the Snow—
        First-Chill—then Stupor—then the letting go . . .

But Oh, let Emily become anything
    but the harp she is, too human, to shiver
        grievous such wracked & torn discord. Let her be

the foam driven before the wind over the lakes,
    over the seas, the powdery glow floating
        the street with evening—saffron, rose, sienna

bricks, matte gold, to be the good steam
    clanking pipes, that warm music glazing the panes,
        each fugitive moment the heaven we choose to make.

MICHAEL KLEIN

Michael Klein is the author of 1990, *a collection of poems, and a memoir,* Track Conditions, *about his race track days. He is also the editor of* Poets for Life: Seventy-Six Poets Respond to AIDS *and (with Marie Howe)* In the Company of My Solitude: American Writing from the AIDS Pandemic. *A native of New York City, Michael Klein teaches at Sarah Lawrence College.*

After the Disease Concept

To say your prayer for being alive
you leave the rehab center each day at noon

and walk in a circle around it to breathe
air that has not been breathed

by twelve recovering alcoholics you left sitting
at your therapy table, trying to grasp

the disease concept.
At the end of the circle, where you sit

beyond a wall of hedges
that keep an unexpected field hidden

your solitude affirms the blissful
inability of staying within a person's reach.

But something botches the meditation
and you think of me

that same uncrystal moment I am thinking
you're dead because there's someone else with your name

in a book of dead names and a number for where you are
in the AIDS quilt

and my desperate message: be alive, is the message
that shakes the snowy edge and moves bright enough

to outlast the shape
of your solitude,

inform your other self. *It's me,* I'm saying.
It's me as my voice.

Yesterday, a Greetings-from-Nevada postcard
arrived of trees dipping their legs

into their origin Lake Tahoe: cocktail music,
twilight. And scribbled right over the picture: alive.

We do survive what isn't in the picture
of our own making, our own words writing our own

history: what we keep seeing, we send.
What we see to keep, we keep.

AIDS, AIDS, AIDS, AIDS, AIDS

In the liberal New York newspaper there are ads
for tans and futons like culture crumbs on the road
to oblivion, or is it ruin? Dirty hands
holding a newspaper—fingerprints on everything.

In the liberal New York newspaper is an article
about the AIDS conference and a review of *Raising Cain,*
the new DePalma film: experimental, it says—the way
they used to talk about Warhol, Robert Downey, and early
Altman—the way we used to talk about schools.

Experiments are over. The monster has walked
out of the hole underground, pre-dawn, pre-sentence
into a preface for the world. AIDS is working.

We were talking about the names.

J. and I were talking about the first unraveling
of quilt names—that gigantic future-is-here-spool
unthreading over the Washington Capitol Lawn. We were
talking about how we talk as much about the death of someone
as we do about the life. We were talking about a vacation
together, away from this sandy arm. We were talking about
getting away for a while—from life.

Signs in the street confound me.
Boots and underwear and pearls confound me. This is a
popular uniform in the gay resort. What does it mean?
Like a Porter lyric, artifice is only affect when it reveals
something about the time. What lyric,

what lyric, what lyric, what lyric, what lyric,
what lyric is this?

JOAN LARKIN

Joan Larkin, who lives in New York City, is the author of several collections of poems, including Housework, A Long Sound, *and* Cold River. *"We live now with such loss, damage, heroism," she writes. "Everything I know has changed—love, community, work, desire. The weight of every day. No surprise, then, that our poems and the stories we tell have changed, too."*

Inventory

One who lifted his arms with joy, first time across the finish
    line at the New York marathon, six months later a skeleton
    falling from threshold to threshold, shit streaming
    from his diaper,
one who walked with a stick, wore a wellcut suit to the
    opera, to poetry readings, to mass, who wrote the best
    long poem of his life at Roosevelt Hospital and read it on
    television
one who went to 35 funerals in 12 months,
one who said *I'm sick of all you AIDS widows,*
one who lost both her sisters,
one who said *I'm not sure that what he and I do is safe, but we're*
    young, I don't think we'll get sick,
one who dying said *They came for me in their boat, they want me*
    on it, and I told them Not tonight, I'm staying here with James,
one who went to Mexico for laetrile,
one who went to California for Compound Q,
one who went to Germany for extract of Venus's flytrap,
one who went to France for humane treatment,
one who chanted, holding hands in a circle,
one who ate vegetables, who looked in a mirror and said *I*
    forgive you,
one who refused to see his mother,
one who refused to speak to his brother,
one who refused to let a priest enter his room,
one who did the best paintings of his life and went home
    from his opening in a taxi with twenty kinds of flowers,
one who moved to San Francisco and lived two more years,
one who married his lover and died next day,
one who said *I'm entirely filled with anger,*
one who said *I don't have AIDS, I have something else,*
one with night sweats, nausea, fever, who worked as a nurse,
one who kept on studying to be a priest,
one who kept on photographing famous women,

one who kept on writing vicious reviews,
one who kept going to AA meetings till he couldn't walk,
one whose son came just once to the hospital,
one whose mother said This is God's judgment,
one whose father held him when he was frightened,
one whose minister said *Beth and her lover of twelve years were
    devoted as Ruth and Naomi*,
one whose clothes were thrown in the street, beautiful shirts
    and ties a neighbor picked from the garbage and handed
    out at a party,
one who said *This room is a fucking prison*,
one who said *They're so nice to me here*,
one who cut my hair and said *My legs bother me*,
who one couldn't stand, who said *I like those earrings*,
one with a tube in his chest, who asked *What are you eating?*
one who said *How's your writing? Are you moving to the moun-
    tains?* who said *I hope you get rich*.
one who said *Death is transition*,
one who was doing new work, entirely filled with anger,
one who wanted to live till his birthday, and did.

Althea

The baby lasted one whole year.
He lay there in the coma, lips like a little knot.
I went after work and bathed him.
I always talked to him.
Then my twin got the virus
and looked it, a skeleton
in a red scarf. Althea,
she'd say, I'm going to die.
And I'd say No.
By then I was sober,
but my brain was on fire:
I'd put my head in the toilet
and flush—ten, fifteen times—
the water was so cold.
My mother'd say when I came
home from my son, Althea,
how do you do it?
I didn't know she was asking
for herself How do you lose

your child? And I didn't answer,
I didn't know then
how the dead live.
Only how to sponge
my son's delicate ribs
my twin's skinny thighs
sweating in the white sheet.
Only how to grab one day
by the wrists and hold on,
whatever is on its breath.

Review

It wasn't the worst movie
I've seen about AIDS.
Lots of nice family.
Catholics who never flinch
from kissing their infected son.
Nobody saying Do you mind
not holding the baby,
not even the pregnant sister
says I love you, but I can't let you
inject yourself in our house.
Not once does the father cry
Where did we go wrong?
Red ribbon looped in every lapel,
no one afraid their faggot
son will burn for eternity.
No one too queer,
no one crazed from death
after death. No kissing,
nothing scarier than a glimpse
of KS sores like a map
of new islands under
the hero's immaculate shirt.
He's a boyscout who once had sex
in a porn theatre, went there
three times in his life—
no 900 numbers,
subway toilets, sadism,
anger, failure, complexity—
it's a movie, isn't it?

How could I expect him
not to die the minute he says
I'm ready—no weeks
of morphine & oxygen, whispers
at the bedside all night,
exhausted laughter, pleading:
You've got to leave your body;
there's nothing left for it but pain.
It was a six-dollar entertainment,
popcorn spilled in the aisles.
But somewhere in the middle, a scene
in a library. The unshaven
gaunt face, the cheap
watch cap, were yours, Denis.
I saw you staring, stripped
to your fear & wanting to live.
And later, listening to Callas,
the dying man's lifted face
flickering green, red—
pleasure, dementia. Love,
it was your face, & I wept.

Waste Not

We're using every bit of your death.
We're making a vise of your mouth's clenching and loosening,
an engine of your labored breathing,
a furnace of your wide-open eyes.

We've reduced you to stock, fed you to the crowd,
banked the pearl of your last anger,
stored the honey of your last smile.

Nothing's left in your mirror,
nothing's floating on your high ceiling.
We're combing pockets, turning sleeves,
shaking out bone and ash,
stripping you down to desire.

Your beloved has folded your house into his—
I'm wading in the Swift River, balancing on stones.

TIMOTHY LIU

Timothy Liu is the author of Burnt Offerings *and* Vox Angelica, *which won the 1992 Norma Farber First Book Award of the Poetry Society of America. He lives in Mt. Vernon, Iowa. "For some," he writes, "sex has brought the gift of life and love. For others, death. How to live in these times is what art at its best tries to answer."*

SFO / HIV / JFK

I knew his job was more than cleaning up
the men's room, waiting for the next man to come
to the polished seat he shined with his spit.
Call it my lucky day, my flight touching
down on an icy runway, wheels skidding
into the unmarked safety of a warm
terminal. I dropped my pants straight off
that long connecting flight to a city
I'd never know, except in passing through.
His city. He showed me pictures: a wife
he met in high school, two sons who attend.
He showed me this in an office downstairs,
having caught my attention with his flashing
pen, toilet paper scrolled up onto it,
had scrawled *I like to suck, get sucked, and fuck.*
If your mother tells you love is decent,
don't believe her, until she tells the truth.
Understand me when I say I didn't
do it for sex. I did it for pity.
For the hundreds of men that I have loved
in airports, busstops, truckstops, interstate
reststops, shopping malls, locker rooms
and janitorial closets, wherever there's enough
room for two men to stand up face to face.
Don't ask me what it's like to go on
living, at first a high priest breaking bread
for hundreds of open mouths, finally
feeding myself in some airport snack bar,
smell of a stranger's sex on my fingers.

DONNA MASINI

Donna Masini's That Kind of Danger *received the 1993 Barnard New Women Poets Prize. She lives in New York City, where she teaches at Hunter College and at the Writer's Voice. "On a very practical level," she writes, "there have been periods of time when I've had to put my work aside—whether due to lack of heart or lack of time. When I have worked on poems, I've been aware of an acute sense of loss that informs everything I write, an awareness of the ways I have failed friends, sustained friends. More and more I see the way I make use of the act of writing to remain present, to see, and perhaps to sustain myself."*

Beauty

for Steven Festa 1953–1987

The optometrist hands me a polaroid of my eye.
I watch as the black circle fades
to a veiny planet. A fetus in its nebular sac.
The branched arteries connect to the optic
nerve where the veins cross.
He can tell a lot from the eye.
He knows what to look for—
thick lines the sign of hardening.
Mine are thin. Healthy. Beautiful, he says.

I have never thought myself beautiful,
one of the blessed who can look steady
at their own reflection, so I was surprised
when you called me beautiful.
It was summer. I was glowing.
You were almost bald. Your face
newly old. Hospital eyes, the color of waiting.
I'd brought you a mechanical dog,
wedges of melon, slivers of ginger for your throat.
I sat by your bed, by your wires and cards
and the pale green wall that could not save you,
almost obscene in my health.
You look beautiful, you said.
I laughed. I can always laugh.
I made you laugh.
I promised to visit.

I hid from your dying. It waited
for me, blew through the valves of me,
pressed itself into faces on subways,

into windows, clean towels, menus. I hid
from it as I was hidden from deaths as a child.
The floating goldfish plucked from their tanks,
flushed down toilets where they turned and surfaced
in rank dreams. You loved animals, held them—
birds, fish, lizards, dogs—as they died in your living
rooms. Sometimes I think beauty is the way you look
on as something you love fades, disintegrates,
the way you wait for the moment when the life blinks out
and what you love has slipped from its skin.
I wrote. You called. I played your voice
back. *No regrets, girl. Never*
any regrets. You're beautiful.
Your voice was blurry. I'd heard you were blind.

How much can the eye take in?
I think it must be the organ of feeling.
I could not look at you
looking at me. What a relief
to touch you, as though my hand
on your chest defined a boundary between us.
Now you were blind.
You would leave the world in pieces
and one of my eyes would begin that long turning
inward, as I came to see what I'd refused.

DAVID MATIAS

Originally from Texas, David Matias lives now in Provincetown, Massachusetts, where he was a 1994–1995 Writing Fellow at the Fine Arts Work Center. He writes: "I move slowly and carefully. I stay alert. All my senses are heightened. I walk with awareness, balancing fear and faith."

Some Things Shouldn't Be Written

During my battle with mycobacterium avium intracellulare,
withering me to 102 pounds—my 7th grade weight—
we finally made an appointment with our lawyer friend.

Even while recovering from the noxious infection,
I never imagined I'd see (at the age of 32) my name embossed
on documents, coupled with *Last Will and Testament.*

We were going to meet the attorney months earlier, but amid
that postcard-perfect summer of '93 we procrastinated.
Both afraid, we made no room to house those intentions.

Messy funeral topics put aside like dirty dishes in the sink.
My stable health offered us a somewhat false sense of peace.
What we wanted least, placed at the bottom of our To Do list.

But by the time the autumn delivered the first birth of cold air,
the cream-colored, legal-sized envelope arrived. Once
cylindrical in my P.O. box, it now lay flat on our kitchen table,

filled with my wishes. As I read the Durable Power of Attorney,
the directives devoted to my memorial service,
each request, each phrase, took my air away.

Small shocks like when my cat's hind paws punch me,
using my stomach as a launching pad to higher space.
In order to calm the startle, I tell myself, *Just breathe deep.*

One night, days before the appointment,
I gave you permission to be as scared as I was.
With your torso shuddering (just like when you chuckle)

mimicking a pillow shook into its pillow case, you said,
I don't want you to die, Davey. . . . Chins served as funnels;
our arms got wet from holding one another. We sat serious

in her office and made decisions as tough as tearing glass.
I appointed you as my Executor. Tension like wallpaper.
We jumped at every opportunity to make feeble jokes.

But rolling back from her desk, in a tall leather chair,
she whispered through a long sigh, *I hate this*.
The hardest question. Our answer: *Cremation*.

In the car you turned on the windshield wipers.
I said, *Wasn't so bad*. You stayed quiet as I watched
the apparent wind push those animated raindrops.

Jerking, they crawl up the margins of the window
and engulf other clear beads like amoebas. They
increase in momentum, eventually flying off

and over the metal roof, flung to God knows where.

Future Senses

The rubber tourniquet tightens by the time
the second vial of blood is drawn.
The muscles that connect my fingers and my wrist begin to cramp.
I'd compare it to Jesus and his palms in pain,
but I know the Romans crucified
through the *carpi*—small bones in the wrist.
By the third vial, I tell the P.A. my hand hurts.
Just one more, he promises. With the fourth vial,

I'm back in Texas, with Elaine.
We move to the kitchen, the way that people at parties do,
holding our half-empty glasses.
We sit on the linoleum floor, backs against the cabinets.
Elaine says our squatting reminds her of her days on heroin.
She explains the steps she used when getting high:
After the tourniquet was on,
I'd slap my arm to protrude a vein.
Her two fingers come down hard, just below

her elbow's wrinkle, and a blood vessel pops—
She's back: she can't believe it, how she's fooled
her body with drug memories; she keeps saying, *Wow, wow.* . . .

Now I stare at four vacutainer tubes
that hold a deep red that belongs to me.
The body knows, like a machine it knows,
it remembers when something bad was put in
and when something good was taken out.
When I wake the next morning
my arm is sore. When I remove the Band-Aid,
there's a small perfect stain on the cotton ball—
dry blood, almost brown, once moist and blue inside my veins.
Still in bed, I look at shadows on thin curtains.
Leaves, barely shielding sunlight.
We are like those shadows, those flat leaves
on material. Forgetting those other parts of us,
so full beyond this world.

RICHARD McCANN

Richard McCann is the author, most recently, of Ghost Letters, which received the 1994 Beatrice Hawley Award and the 1993 Capricorn Poetry Prize. He divides his time between Provincetown, Massachusetts, and Washington, D.C., where he co-directs the graduate creative writing program at American University. He writes: "On Pearl Harbor Day 1984, my lover, Jaime, was informed he was HIV-positive. He called me from Sacramento, where he'd gotten sick on a business trip, to tell me the news. For a long time afterwards, I felt afraid of what had once seemed "perfect bodies"—men's bodies at the gym, for instance, bodies from which even the idiosyncratic irregularities of pubic hair had been 'repaired' and 'cosmeticized'; bodies that seemed sculpted from marble, as if in order to defeat everything, including personality and time. For a long time, that is, the coveted body, like desire, seemed a door to grief. Eleven years later, when Jaime died, I knew that he was very beautiful to me, although he weighed less than a hundred pounds, and his skin tore and bled wherever anyone touched it. I have felt a responsibility to write about this—to embody this experience, as it were, in the midst of loss."

Nights of 1990

"The sweatings and the fevers stop, the throat that was unsound
is sound, the lungs of the consumptive are resumed. . . ."
—WALT WHITMAN, *"The Sleepers"*

1.
What I could not accept was how much space
his body was taking with it: for instance, the space where
I was standing, the dazed fluorescence of his hospital room
where each night I watched him sleep. *So this*
is the spine, I thought, this articulation
of vertebral tumors, this rope of bulbous knots;
tissue, I thought, as I studied his yellowing skin—
tissue, like something that could tear.
Afterward, I waited in the corridor.
When I came back, he was alive and breathing.
Here, let me rub your back, I said.
Was it true what I'd heard, that the soul resides in breath?
Was it true the body was mere transport? I untied
the white strings that secured his pale blue
hospital gown. The blue gown drifted
from his shoulders. I rubbed his back.
I rubbed his back. *Not so hard,*
he said. *I don't need to be burnished yet.*

2.
Tonight I am loyal to the young men in leather jackets loitering
by the lighted windows of the Churrería San Sebastian. To Manuel
Mendoza Hernandez de Gato, one name for each day I loved him,
Patron Saint of Cafe-Bar Lolita and the gypsy caves of Sacromonte. To Juan
Francisco Gomez de Zamora, to the black stars and coiled serpents
tattooed to his hands. Tonight I am loyal to the Bar With No Name.

Each night that summer I stood by a path that transected *El Retiro*,
a park whose dangers the police patrolled. Tiers of streetlamps
silvered terraces of ornamental roses, the vast statuary
of a crystal palace abandoned during war. If memory

could build its own monument to that moment
—There was a field by the train station, well-known
among a certain kind. Past midnight I knelt
in the wet uncut grass, sheltered
by the man who stood before me.
He quickly came. He zipped his trousers.
He stroked my face. *Mi amigo,*
he whispered, *I have a favor to ask.*
Will you suck off my friend?

Yes, I said. *I will suck off your friend.*

3.
What was it you said?
Better to pass boldly into that other world, in the full glory
of some passion . . .

Here, let me touch your face again.
Your face, in the full glory of some passion.

When the bleeding woman touched Christ's garment
and straightaway the source of her blood was dried up
so that He felt the virtue going out of Him to heal her—
why did He turn in the crowd to demand
Who touched my clothes?

The disciples said:
Thou seest the multitude
thronging thee, and sayest thou,
Who touched me?

I remember those nights.
It was dark. You traced your name on my bare chest.

When you straddled my hips and rose above me
I knew I had no choice but
to submit to touch again, I knew I'd have to endure
this wish forever. The long line of your spine
looked like a scar perfectly sealed.

4.
In my dream, you were alive. You had been dead.
To prove it, your arms were cut off at the elbows.

We were in a factory basement. Someone was whispering,
A terrible, terrible accident. You showed me your bandages.
Then you told me: *I'm ready to go home now. Home,*

I thought. *Where was home?* Only later did I realize you'd been
through fire. The next morning when I dressed for work,
that is, I saw the silver vase that holds your ashes,
and I realized you had no body, no body at all;
you were less than even the word *body*.
Sleeping, I had believed you were a ghost, maybe—

Ghost of a chance. I still loved you.
Then why in the dream did I leave you? And why did I say
I would never go back—not ever—to the room where you sat
touching yourself with your bandaged arms? *Touch me,*
you pleaded. But you were not restored. You would never be whole.

5.
And you, God, if you were to speak to me now
through his body—his reckless body; his tender, feathered
body; his fragile body that even in its dying sometimes
seemed newborn, so compassionate and astonishing . . .

Or through that other body, the body I saw in the street,
trousers down around its shit-smeared ass, flies
swarming over; bleeding, half-conscious body; Christ's body
—if Christ were old, and despicable . . .

Here, let me hold your body against this clean white linen;

here, let me hold your body against myself, a stranger's body
I might one night have drunkenly borne
—your come on my chest, my mouth. Dear God,

in your dearness, what were you but each night's longing
shaped by a stranger's touch? And what was I
but the agent of that longing cast to earth
to fend for us both? Was it your sin if you felt unloved?

Here, let me comb your hair before you die . . .

Here, press your body to this white sheet, the miraculous imprint . . .

What was it men used to tell me?
Sure, I'll call you. Leave your number on the dresser.

I read somewhere, a friend said, *that in the old days
the saints actually prayed for wounds. Can you imagine
actually praying to have wounds?*

Yes, I imagined myself saying. *I can imagine praying for wounds.*
Of course I was tired. Of course I wanted to get home.
Like many others, I was trying to hail a taxi.

When you were dying a woman came to your room.
I couldn't tell if she was the janitor or the chaplain. She said
there was a miracle occurring among us at that very moment.

In this lime green room? I thought.
In this lime green room? How perfectly horrible.

She straightened the pillows. She built a pyramid
from the miniature juice cans you'd left on your windowsill.
I thought, *So this is what one does to prepare for a miracle.*

One the door to your room a discreet white sign warned: *Caution. Bodily fluids.*

(You whispered: "Long I was hugg'd close—long and long.")

In *The New York Times* surgeons were discussing their fears of bodily fluids:

"Every so often you take off your gloves and your fingers are covered with blood."

*"I can't count how many times my arms were covered with blood.
I can't count how many pairs of shoes and socks I soaked and ruined."*

When the hospital therapist asked me what was the matter
I told him my heart had broken. He placed his hands on my chest.
He said, "Now I'm going to press down harder."

That final glorious spring Saturday. You said,
Let's take a walk around the neighborhood and see who's dying.

On your wrist an infant's blue plastic bracelet warned: *Caution. Bodily fluids.*

("Long I was hugg'd close—long and long.")

Late that night, on the way home from the hospital,
I stopped for a Coke at a 7-11 where there was a robbery in progress.
Three boys were filling a paper bag with cash
and powdered donuts. *Your money or your life,*

they were joking with the customers, who wouldn't budge from line.
Evidently the customers were people who'd all been robbed before.
—All but one who was hiding by the freezer case, that is, the one
who was crying. The customers were yelling at him: *Shut up!*

Can't you see you're scaring us to death? Really,
he was frightful, with KS lesions on his face, and his hair
mostly fallen out. *I refuse to die,*
he was crying. *I refuse to die in this 7-11.*

Once, sitting in your hospital room, I told you
I had wanted a man to touch me
in a way that would feel like "forever."

It wasn't that I didn't die trying, you said.

You, come here. Sit beside me. I'm not that unhappy.
After all, not even a touch of faith lasts forever.
And, after all, it's true that what life gave me sometimes proved
enough: its simple, loving,

courteous touch—which could have been yours,
or a stranger's, or even the masseur's
as he pressed his hands between my shoulder blades
and whispered *Breathe,*
Breathe deeply,
Why do you keep forgetting to breathe?

After You Died

I had a body again. And I could recall
how it had been, back then,

to want: things. Easy to recall that now—
this sun-dazed room; lilacs, in white bowls.
But for a long time I was grateful
only for what your dying was taking from me:
the world, dismantling itself; soon there'd be no more obstinacies,
I wouldn't want anything again . . .

After you died I rode a bicycle around the lake all day, in circles.
I had come back. And so it was hard not to remember
how it had been walking the path that circled the lake
where I'd once gone each night to look for sex.
It's true that I drank heavenly

—*heavily*, I mean. I was drunk.
I walked until someone wanted me. But what did I hope
to love in return?—I followed him, his pale shirt disappearing
into a small clearing hidden by shrubs.
He undressed, his bare chest mottled by moonlight's shadows of leaves.
If I could have followed you like that, even in grief,
into a clearing littered with wadded paper tissues
                                        —white carnations!

Mostly I met no one.
The path ended by the public toilets.
I loitered by a row of urinals; or I stood outside,
beneath the dim, caged streetlamp,
in a body I hated. Without it,
who'd need to ask the world for a thing?

JAMES MERRILL

James Merrill was born in New York City and lived in Stonington, Connecticut. He was the author of twelve books of poems, including Nights and Days, *which received the National Book Award;* Braving the Elements, *which received the Bollingen Prize in Poetry;* Divine Comedies, *which won the Pulitzer Prize;* The Changing Light at Sandover; *and* A Scattering of Salts, *which was published after his death in February 1995. He was also the author of two prose works,* Recitative *and* A Different Person, *a memoir.*

Tony: Ending the Life

Let's die like Romans,
Since we have lived like Grecians.

—VOLPONE

Across the sea at Alexandria,
Shallow and glittering, a single shroud-
Shaped cloud had stolen, leaving as it paused
The underworld dilated, a wide pupil's
Downward shaft. The not-yet-to-be mined
Villa, a fortune of stone cards each summer
Less readable, more crushing, lay in wait
Beneath the blue-green sand of the sea floor.
Plump in schoolboy shorts, you peered and peered.
For wasn't youth like that—its deep charades
Revealed to us alone by passing shades?
But then years, too, would pass. And in the glow
Of what came next, the Alexandria
You brought to life would up and go:
Bars, beaches, British troops (so slim—yum yum!)
The parties above all. Contagious laughter,
Sparkle and hum and flow,
Saved you from weighty insights just below;
Till from another shore
(Folégandros, the western end of Crete)
Age, astonished, saw those heavy things
Lifted by tricky prisms into light,
Lifted like holy offerings,
Gemlike, disinterested,
Within the fleet
Reliquary of wave upon wave as it crested.

One year in Athens I let my beard grow.
The locals took it for a badge of grief.

Had someone died? Not yet, I tried to joke.
Of course beards came in every conceivable format—
Dapper, avuncular, deadbeat . . .
Mine warned of something creepier—uh-oh!
For over throat and lips had spread a doormat
On which to wipe filth brought in from the street.

Unfair! The boys were talkative and fun;
Far cleaner than my mind, after a bath.
Such episodes, when all was said and done,
Sweetened their reflective aftermath:
The denizens discovered in a dive
Relieved us (if not long or overmuch).
"Just see," the mirror breathed, "see who's alive,
Who hasn't forfeited the common touch,

The longing to lead everybody's life"
—Lifelong daydream of precisely those
Whom privilege or talent set apart:
How to atone for the achieved uniqueness?
By dying everybody's death, dear heart—
Saint, terrorist, fishwife. Stench that appals.
Famines, machine guns, the Great Plague (your sickness),
Rending of garments, cries, mass burials.

I'd watched my beard sprout in the mirror's grave.
Mirrors *are* graves, as all can see:
Knew this emerging mask would outlast me,
Just as the life outlasts us, that we led . . .
And then one evening, off it came. No more
Visions of the deep. These lines behave
As if we were already gone—not so!
Although of course each time's a closer shave.

One New Year's Eve, on midnight's razor stroke,
Kisses, a round of whiskies. You then drew
Forth from your pocket a brightness, that season's new
Two drachma piece, I fancied, taking the joke
—But no. Proud of your gift, you warned: "Don't leave
The barman this. Look twice." My double take
Lit on a grave young fourteen-carat queen
In profile. Heavens preserve us! and long live

Orbits of Majesty whereby her solar
Metal sets the standard. (A certain five-dollar
Piece, redeemed for paper—astute maneuver—
Taught me from then on: don't trust Presidents.)
Here it buys real estate. From the packed bus's
Racket and reek a newly-struck face glints
No increment of doubt or fear debases.
Speaking of heavens, Maria, a prime mover

In ours, one winter twilight telephoned:
Not for you to see her so far gone,
But to pick up, inside the unlatched door,
A satchel for safe keeping. *Done and done*,
You called from home to say. But such a weight,
Who lifted it? No one. She'd had to kick,
Incy by inch, your legacy down the hall,
The heavy bag of gold, her setting sun.

The sea is dark here at day's end
And the moon gaunt, half-dead
Like an old woman—like Madame Curie
About her vats of pitchblende
Stirred dawn to dusk religiously
Out in the freezing garden shed.

It is a boot camp large and stark
To which you will be going.
Wave upon wave of you. The halls are crowded,
Unlit, the ceiling fixtures shrouded.
Advancing through the crush, the matriarch
Holds something up, mysteriously glowing.

Fruit of her dream and labor, see, it's here
(See too how scarred her fingertips):
The elemental sliver
Of matter heading for its own eclipse
And ours—this "lumière de l'avenir"
Passed hand to hand with a faint shiver:

Light that confutes the noonday blaze.
A cool uncanny blue streams from her vial,
Bathing the disappearers
Who asked no better than to gaze and gaze . . .

Too soon your own turn came. Denial
No longer fogged the mirrors.

You stumbled forth into the glare—
Blood-red ribbon where you'd struck your face.
Pills washed down with ouzo hadn't worked.
Now while the whole street buzzed and lurked
The paramedics left you there,
Returning costumed for a walk in Space.

The nurse thrust forms at you to sign,
Then flung away her tainted pen.
. . . . Lie back now in that heat
Older than Time, whose golden regimen
Still makes the palm grow tall and the date sweet . . .
Come, a last sip of wine.

Lie back. Over the sea
Sweeps, faint at first, the harpist's chord.
Purple with mourning, the royal barge gasps nearer.
Is it a test? a triumph? No more terror:
How did your namesake, lovesick Antony,
Meet the end? By falling on his sword

—A story in Plutarch
The plump boy knew from History class.
Slowly the room grows dark.
Stavro who's been reading you the news
Turns on a nightlight. No more views.
Just your head, nodding off in window-glass.

RON MOHRING

Ron Mohring lives in Houston, Texas, and is a student in the graduate writing program at Vermont College. " 'The Useful Machine' is dedicted to my partner of ten years, David Wright, who died in January 1995," he writes. "The poem came about as I was grappling with this approaching loss. It seemed to me that one way to face what was happening might be to write my way into it, to imagine the other side where I would be alone, and so come to terms with the inevitable. The reality, of course, was like nothing I'd imagined, like nothing I'd lived through."

The Useful Machine

Look at the
useful machine I built instead of grieving.
—RACHEL WETZSTEON

Programmed to operate without commands, this amazing unit
practically thinks for itself. Sensitive as the delicate, twitchy hands

of a Geiger counter, but more discreet—no blinks, no whistles
nor bells—it efficiently searches and finds the particular stimuli

invisibly linked to my suggestible moods. It reads my mind
like a map. Better than. In short, it *knows.* The sun this afternoon

blares through the blinds, backlights the Easter cactus that still grows,
despite neglect, on the table. The light reveals the plant's insides—

a central spine—and shows the thinnest ribs. Before I know
what I feel, before I'm able to think the word *x-ray*, a Sousa march

intended to conceal the image I recall
snaps on in my brain. I override, remember anyway:

I'd lie beside x in the narrow bed too small for both of us,
and lightly place my head against his chest. A monitor in the wall

would beep at brief intervals as it fed what x's nurse had dubbed
his "grocery list." I liked the way she smiled, how once she said

Now that's a cozy picture. A green tank hissed its careful load of oxygen.
She had a voice like Elmer Fudd's, the nurse, a Miss Lamar. She walked

with a prominent limp. I'd forgotten her voice. Of course, it's this
machine: it won't let me feel sad. Adroit, it manages phone calls, intercepts

well-meaning friends who drop by unannounced
to cook and clean, who feel obliged to force me into chatter:

the weather, which teams were trounced in the NFL. They're worse
than television. But I refuse to be bounced on the knees of the kind.

I'll make my own decisions. I'm tired of hearing the same advice
delivered by people who don't even grasp my situation:

*Is it feed a cold and starve a fever or starve a cold and feed
a fever?* Feed a man who burns with fever, feed his fever,

feel how cold then hot his body speeds through cycles like a washer,
wringing out the sweat. His bony frame chattered like clothespins

stuck to a twanging line. Forget yourself. Forget your needs,
or think of them constantly, but go without. Careen from hope to doubt

and back again. Let someone wish you luck; then wonder what the words
intend. They say a silver cord connects the soul, a plucky astronaut

spacewalking—mother-may-I?—snaking out on tiptoe but then
with giant steps, as if to run away. The precise moment the tether

breaks is when the body's lost. Soul floats free, a snapped kite.
I'm speaking once again of x. I wanted him to die, to be

unchangeable. The machine is a lie. I planned to help if I had to.
What does this make me?

PAUL MONETTE

Paul Monette died of AIDS-related complications in February 1995, at the age of forty-nine. He was the author of four collections of poems and six novels, as well as three important and influential nonfiction prose works, Borrowed Time: An AIDS Memoir; Becoming a Man: Half a Life Story; *and* Last Watch of the Night. *In addition to the National Book Award, he received the PEN Center West Freedom to Write Award, three Lambda Literary Awards, honorary Doctor of Letters degrees from Wesleyan University and the City University of New York, and numerous civic awards for political activism in the fight against AIDS. In his introduction to* Love Alone: 18 Elegies for Rog, *he wrote: "These elegies were written during the five months after [my beloved friend] died, one right after the other, with hardly a half day's pause between. Writing them quite literally kept me alive, for the only time I wasn't wailing and trembling was when I was hammering at these poems. I have let them stand as raw as they came . . . . I want them to allow no escape, like a hospital room, or indeed a mortal illness."*

Here

everything extraneous has burned away
this is how burning feels in the fall
of the final year not like leaves in a blue
October but as if the skin were a paper lantern
full of trapped moths beating their fired wings
and yet I can lie on this hill just above you
a foot beside where I will lie myself
soon soon and for all the wrack and blubber
feel still how we were warriors when the
merest morning sun in the garden was a
kingdom after Room 1010 war is not all
death it turns out war is what little
thing you hold on to refugeed and far from home
oh sweetie will you please forgive me this
that every time I opened a box of anything
Glad Bags One-A-Days KINGSIZE was
the worst I'd think will you still be here
when the box is empty Rog Rog who will
play boy with me now that I bucket with tears
through it all when I'd cling beside you sobbing
you'd shrug it off with the quietest *I'm still
here* I have your watch in the top drawer
which I don't dare wear yet help me please
the boxes grocery home day after day
the junk that keeps men spotless but it doesn't
matter now how long they last or I

the day has taken you with it and all
there is now is burning dark the only green
is up by the grave and this little thing
of telling the hill I'm here oh I'm here

Manifesto

unsolicited Adam S diagnosed 9/85
and lucky calls to say all sickness is self-
induced and as I start to growl oozes self-
beatification *taking a course in miracles*
he says and I bark my way out of his wee
kirk and savage his name from the Rolodex
another triumph of self-love like metaphysical
sit-ups a washboard ripple on the pre-
frontal lobe doubtless the work of Mrs. Hay
baghwan of the leper set Pooh-bear in hand
purveying love-is-you with an anchorlady's
do and Diane Arbus eyes straight-faced told
a reporter people in train wrecks bring it on
themselves *But what if somebody gets the virus
from a transfusion* WHAT ARE THEY DOING NEEDING
BLOOD IN THE FIRST PLACE pounces Lady Hay
every sucker in the ICU's to blame see
there are no microbes just self-loathing come
sit in a ring with St. Louise and deep-throat
your pale sore body lick your life like a dog's
balls and repeat after me I AM A MIRACLE
why do I care about all this who does it
harm shouldn't the scared and solo have a shot
at warding it off six months a year by dint
of mellowness well yes and no we need
the living alive to bucket Ronnie's House
with abattoirs of blood hand in hand lesions
across America need to trainwreck the whole
show till someone listens so no they may not
coo in mirrors disbarring the fevered the choked
and wasting as losers who have not learned
like Adam the yoga with which to kiss their own
asshole every tent revival mantra
is one less bomb tossed in the red-taped labs
of the FDA one less bureaucrat pelted

as he chews his Pilate's thumb toddling home
by limo to Silver Springs where all high-risk
behavior is curfewed after dusk forget it
the boys at Mrs. Hay's haven't an anarchist
bone in their spotted torsos miraculized
they may be but even if they last forever
will only love the one poor thing themself
and bury the rest of us spring in their stride
as they whistle home with the shovel thinking
I'm still here the level earth wide as they
can see strewn with burn and ruin like a
crash site but I admit it I love you better
than me Rog always have you're no different
all the migrainous interchange with crooks
and fools lines at the post that inch like Poland
dogged nerves of a day's wage how much self
is functional by Thursday afternoon unless
it has a weekend place remote as Na Pali
green as the light on Daisy's dock the boys
of Hay are learning how to laugh again
but what if one never forgot in the first
place oh boys I warn you now joy alone
will not protect you have it all you can
life if you have to say you believe in
Oral Roberts's eighty-foot Jesus with
the ransom note but keep your miracles small
my friend and I we laughed for years on end
and the dark fell anyway and all our people
sicken and have no rage the Feds are lying
about the numbers the money goes for toilet
seats in bombers the State of the Union
is pious as Pius washing his hands of Hitler
Jews are not a Catholic charity when is
enough enough I had a self myself
once but he died when do we leave the mirror
and lie down in front of the tanks let them
put two million of us away see how quick
it looks like Belsen force out all their hate
the cool indifferent genocide that locks up
all the pills whatever it takes witness
the night and the waste for those who are not yet
touched for soon the thing will ravish their women
their jock sons lie in rows in the empty infield

the scream in the streets will rise to a siren din
and they will beg us to teach them how to
bear it we who are losing our reason

The Bee-Eater

We walk on air, Watson.
—SYLVIA PLATH

For Carol Muske

The killer bees—Africanized—have reached San Diego
and I got a C– in Elementary Sci.
New evidence every day that I wasted my youth
on English Lit. That is, I don't know shit
about pollination or why bugs are our friends.
Not that I haven't followed them north
year by year, valley by valley, bearing
the beaded sungod of El Dorado,
the dewdrop gleam of the eagle priests
who heal by sting and pistil. How many times
have I bolted awake with the guilty terror—
the swarm upon me, roaring like a 747.
Once even dreamed I was eating them
like a mouthful of blackberries

                                        taste of

gunmetal and caramel

                            couldn't scream
through the foam of pain

                            A veritable
balloon-man all through my tenth summer, I was
the bees' bullseye. The whole hive courted me—
yellowjackets, blue-bellied hornets, furry
bumbles, two-inch wasps. I drew them like
a rotten plum. By August I was on a steroid
drip. Next year they let me be, and the next
and the next, but you never lose the fear
of buzzing

roses are never the same
                              nor sweets
nor syrup nor even soap. You wash with
oatmeal, chew garlic, dress gray, screen
callers, wander only after dark—

Now I know how an allergy works:
life gives you an A in your own disease.
You take a little venom at a time
and soon you purr with tolerance. Say one
a day, stinger applied directly to the tongue
or sucked like a quivering lozenge.
Self-treatment you'll say is risky:
Jack London OD'd at 40, needling
himself for tropical fevers, and all
the wolves in Yellowknife howled
at the moon in grief
                              but no entomologists

Addiction may occur. Look, the doctors
don't know shit either. The bee-men
got their timetable wrong, and here I am,
not immune enough. If I don't start eating now
they'll be here, covering the house
like a pear tree. Measure my days
by sting if I have to. It's August,
the garden is moaning, we have no
winter to hide in. So bring on the just
desserts, the honey-domed, the dream-
candy kamikaze panacea kiss of death.

Oh bees my bees, come take me.

MARY JANE NEALON

Mary Jane Nealon is a registered nurse and poet living in Provincetown, Massachusetts, where she is a Writing Fellow at the Fine Arts Work Center. Her essay "Realizations at Bedside" appeared in In the Company of My Solitude: American Writing from the AIDS Pandemic. *She writes: "My work has been influenced in the same way my life has been: by a feeling of urgency and compassion toward those who are infected and a desire to make my poetry speak for those who have not yet spoken."*

Watching the Solar Eclipse with AIDS Patients in Infectious Disease Clinic, May 10, 1994

To save our retinas, we slip your x-rays
from the film jacket. Your entire radiographic
history is here. We choose the most recent
picture of your chest, the one with dense
patchy infiltrates, the one where having failed
to remove your gold chain, a small cross
is suspended among rib bones.

We line up, take turns passing the protective
slice of film back and forth. At the moment
when the moon pauses at the center of sun
it has the same heavy black nucleus as the virus.
The ordinary slides out of sight.

Soon the drama has passed, the moon edging
its way along. We are tired of the way
death has waited. It lays its stubborn hand
on the young man with tall stalks of heliconia
across his knees, tulips for all of us in his arms.

The Illustrious Providence of Solid Tumors

"... James Sauderling's mother tould him she bewitched her Cow,
but afterwards said that her Cow should doe well againe, for it
was not her Cow but an Other Person's that should dye."
—Transcript, Salem Witchcraft Trials, 17th century

On the expensive Sony screen, cell clusters are zinnias.
Erratic tumors sliced down like this astound us
with their beauty. The pathologist sits up straight,
explains what will happen. I try to hold onto the idea
of your body: pierced nipples permanently erect,

a dangling half-moon in silver; your well-loved rectum,
your soft testicle sac. Even when he focuses and zooms
the slide, nothing in this clump of tissue
is evocative of you.

I think about the old witch woman,
taking a curse from this cow, putting it on another.
How they *boyled the Heart of a Calfe that Dyed, boyled
the flesh, boyled the bones.* They weighed the bulk
of things. Large meaty pieces of disease.
They took the organs out, even after death,
to cleanse them. This they did by candlelight,
with much twisting of tongues, fits and raising-up.

We take the smallest parts of you: slice and split,
stain, enlarge. We muse over you.
No one will say AIDS, they imagine your cancer
as a separate and pure aberration. We talk of chemo
as though it were the ordinary course of things,
ignore the devastated slack face of your lover
who zips and unzips the leather jacket pocket,
who twirls the beautiful emerald
in your left earlobe with his long ring finger.

The Pathologist Dictates

On the phone to the morgue
I rattle off a list of cultures
we want from your abandoned body:
cryptococcus, toxoplasmosis, aspergillosis.

In the background the pathologist says,
in the most delicate of voices:
Now I am entering the bronchial tree.

All day I imagine this journey.
I swim in a black-bottom pool,
behind a white gate, with sunflowers.
Above me branches open out,
mirror the flowering of our lungs.

In death there is no collapsing
of the final breath, rather a holding-on
of air beneath relaxed and suspended
chest muscles.

When we turn your body,
our careful movements shift
the last air in your bronchioles,
so you emit small sounds:
a timid and still *unsure* singing.

CARL PHILLIPS

Carl Phillips is the author of Cortège *and* In the Blood, *which received the 1992 Morse Poetry Prize from Northeastern University. He lives in St. Louis, where he is professor of English at Washington University. He writes: "It's as if death had been there of course—before the arrival of AIDS and its swift escalation to pandemic—but it was shadowless and therefore easier to forget, if only briefly. Now, with a greater awareness of death, my poems have turned to previously unexplored areas, in particular the matter of devotion (religious and secular, to the living, to the dead) and the thornier issue of how to rethink and reconfigure sexual desire within the same arena as death. I haven't figured it out—I keep writing the poems, as if toward solution."*

As from a Quiver of Arrows

What do we do with the body, do we
burn it, do we set it in dirt or in
stone, do we wrap it in balm, honey,
oil, and then gauze and tip it onto
and trust it to a raft and to water?

What will happen to the memory of his
body, if one of us doesn't hurry now
and write it down fast? Will it be
salt or late light that it melts like?
Floss, rubber gloves, a chewed cap

to a pen elsewhere—how are we to
regard his effects, do we throw them
or use them away, do we say they are
relics and so treat them like relics?
Does his soiled linen count? If so,

would we be wrong, then, to wash it?
There are no instructions whether it
should go to where are those with no
linen, or whether by night we should
memorially wear it ourselves, by day

reflect upon it folded, shelved, empty.
Here, on the floor behind his bed, is
a bent photo—why? Were the two of
them lovers? Does it mean, where we
found it, that he forgot it or lost it

or intended a safekeeping? Should we
attempt to make contact? What if this
other man too is dead? Or alive, but
doesn't want to remember, is human?
Is it okay to be human, and fall away

from oblation and memory, if we forget,
and can't sometimes help it and sometimes
it is all that we want? How long, in
dawns or new cocks, does that take?
What if it is rest and nothing else that

we want? Is it a findable thing, small?
In what hole is it hidden? Is it, maybe,
a country? Will a guide be required who
will say to us how? Do we fly? Do we
swim? What will I do now, with my hands?

Tunnel

> *Come now, if ever.*
> *When it is raining this gentle*
> *and the first thought is of semen,*
> *and the second thought is of lilies*
> *when by their own pale weight*
> *they bend, sing to the ground something,*
> *and the third thought is of*
> *what joy or sadness can be*
> *available to what is finally a lily*
> *and can't sing.*

> :

And you said *It is wind* and *It is heat*,
hearing the doors shift in their frames.
Because you could not say what also
to call it: God as what is relentless,
God as oil, redolent, proffered;
the final, necessary cross-stitch of
death whose meaning is that everything
finds closure; or the meaningless,
already tipped, disembodied scales
in which we are all of us, inescapably,

found wanting, because how can we
not want?

    :

    In the street below, the latest version of cool need, his
    black car shining in such a way as to make all of it (that
    any children around follow, that each longs to see his own
    face given back, and the one boy, that he is chosen, is
    getting in) seem natural, inevitable.

    :

the body, bright thing and holy   *the body as raft-like*
the ocean beneath it as waves   *the waves as many small fans*
the one you loved, he is dead   *the one I love, he is dead*
each wave beneath him is blue   *—blue, collapsing*

    :

—Sunday morning, the Greek diner. The men in pairs from
last night. Again the different, more difficult
tenderness that is two men with only their briefly shared
flesh in common as they eat and don't eat much, together.
At the window *brush/fail, brush/fail* go the leaves.

    :

After Patroklos, impatient, took the armor of Achilles,
after he put it on his own body
and rode into battle, and then died,
Achilles fell into grief—
not for the loss of the armor that was his,
but for love of the man who had last worn it,
who could never, now,
be brought back.
His goddess-mother, Thetis, hearing
as far away as the sea's bottom
his uncontrollable cries, hurried to him.
A lot of words, armor, a new shield . . .

       :

    Here is the sun.
    Take some.
    Here is the rain, in no apparent way
    holy, but serving still.
    Wash.
    Drink.
    Here is the body.
    Do not imagine now balm.
    The wounds are to be
    left open.

for Frank

From the Devotions

I.

As if somewhere, away, a door had slammed shut.
—But not metal; not wood.

Or as when something is later remembered only
as something dark in the dream:

torn, bruised, dream-slow
descending, it could be anything—

tiling, clouds,
you again, beautifully consistent, in no

usual or masterable way   *leaves, a woman's*
shaken-loose throat, shattered

eyes of the seer, palms, ashes, the flesh
instructing; you, silent.

A sky, a sea requires crossing and, like that,
there is a boat or, like that, a plane:

for whom is it this way now, when
as if still did I lie down beside, still

turn to, touch
                    I can't, I could not save you?

II.

Not, despite what you believed, that
all travel necessarily ends here, at the sea.

I am back, but only because.
As the sun only happens to meet the water

in such a way that the water becomes
a kind of cuirass: how each piece takes

and, for nothing, gives back whatever light—
sun's, moon's. A bird that is not a gull

passes over; I mark what you would: underneath,
at the tip of either wing, a fluorescent-white

moon, or round star. Does the bird itself
ever see this? According to you   *many have*

had the ashes of lovers strewn here,
on this beach   on this water that now beats at,

now seems to want just to rest alongside.
The dead can't know we miss them   Presumably,

we were walking   *that we are walking*
upon them.

III.
All night, again,
a wind that failed to bring storm—

instead, the Paradise dream: the abandoned
one nest at a bad angle—in danger,

and what it is to not know it;
the equally abandoned one tree that,

for the time being, holds it—alone,
and what it is to not know it.

All morning, it has been the fog
thinning at last,

as if that were the prayer,
the streets filling with men   *as if they*

were divine answer and not just
what happens. Do I love less, if less is

all I remember? Your mouth, like a hole
to fly through. What you understood

of the flesh: how always first are we
struck down. *Then we rise; are astounded.*

In the Blood, Winnowing

I.
Before the dumb hoof
through the chest, the fine hair
of wire drawn over the head, snapping
free the neck's blue chords,

before the visionary falling away
from a body left mumbling to itself,
consigned to the damp sling
of tropic circumstance,

there was this morning now,
in the shower, when you know
you are dying,

you are dying and your body—
a lozenge or a prayer, whatever goes
slim and unimportant when the tongue
has grown overly zealous—

contracts under the steam,
under the light that shows up on your skin
as a deep red the shower's curtain
alone can't account for.

II.
What is it but
yours, the one hand
drawing the scrotum (no longer
yours) back upon itself?
When you come
into the other hand, it's like
spitting on death's breast, on
her spectator shoes,
to distract her.
Trembling in the water,
in the stick of yourself,
you watch the talisman's shadow,
already twisting, diminished against
the tiles, to the pig's-tail stump
of conclusion,

all it ever was.

III.
Stones do not matter.
You are twenty-nine for no reason,
or thirty-seven, your favorite prime.
Perhaps you are precisely that age
when a writer means, finally,
all that he says, a cubed square
of cell after cell containing
all the hounds of childhood,
with their hard buckles and hot
irons, their pins for under
your fingers. Dreams
are of falling
asleep at locked windows,
you are all the stones
that keep missing the glass.

IV.
Nothing stops
for you admiring the hair
that has sprung late
at either shoulder,
for you crushing your face
into the shirts that bloom
like cutaway views of old
lovers from your wall of closet.
It is any morning when the train
rattles over birdsong, the suggestion
of blades coming dry
from the night; brilliantly,
shaft after shaft, the sun passes
over the shit and bone and feather
of yours and other lives on earth,
the canted row-houses, children
in their crippled victory gardens,
throwing knives in the air,

and you tell yourself (already
growing hard again over the train's
crosstown difficulties)
that everything counts:

the correct tie,
the bit of skin between sock
and cuff, the man beside you,
strange and familiar as a tattoo
the hand wakes to and keeps
wanting to touch,
refusing to believe
in that part of the world
where things don't wash off.

BOYER RICKEL

Boyer Rickel is the author of arreboles, *a book of poems. He lives in Tucson, where he is Assistant Director of the Creative Writing Program at the University of Arizona. He writes: "The experience of AIDS creates a new premise for my life, all parts of my life, which of course includes my writing. It's as pervasive—and as difficult to name—as a change of light when a new season advances. But this change refuses to give way: there seems to be no next season."*

Poem to Begin the Second Decade of AIDS

The dog, alive, Lucy, my light, sleeps
    on the couch I'd have trained her off of
had not someone coaxed her, repeatedly,
    to clamber up, then lie down along
his outstretched legs; Gary, alive, who,

    had he had his way at first, wouldn't
have let her live with us at all for fear
    she'd dig up the bulbs and seedlings,
or strip the bark from young acacias
    and mesquites in our yard alive with

four years of his ceaseless shovel, shoulder,
    rake and sweat. The hour darkens, sweetens,
whenever I ask how long for all of this—
    November lettuces, April poppies, Lucy's
dog-fragrant, humid *hrumph* across my

    rising/falling, almost-sleeping chest,
how long the *chauk, chauk* of Gary's spade,
    the swells and waves of caliche and dust.
This poem is far too private for anybody
    but us. This poem will make certain

close friends blush, who prefer poems be
    like linens they can put in drawers,
sure of their place and use. Today I
    thought of this as I took up our blue
wool blanket, a week-long winter freeze

   having passed, folding once, twice,
a cloudless, geometrically diminishing sky;
   then twice again, all compact, tangible
potential, ready to unfold and warm or
   simply drape across a reclining form.

January 1990

JEROD SANTEK

Before moving to Minneapolis, Jerod Santek worked for several years with HIV/AIDS educational and service organizations in San Francisco, Phoenix, and Washington, D.C. His poems have appeared in such magazines as Ploughshares *and* The James White Review. *He writes: "My poetry comes as much from my professional experience with HIV/AIDS as it does from my personal experiences, motivated by the need to gain a better understanding of what I encountered each day. When writing about HIV/AIDS, I increasingly turn to formal poetry. I find the constraints placed by the forms allow me to focus more and keep me in control, which is a welcomed feeling when writing about subjects that feel so out of control."*

HIV Research Project

She tells me it's a simple procedure
as she places a pad above my eye.
She warns me I cannot move; the slightest
movement is registered and the whole trial
has to be thrown out. "Focus on something
close to the ground so your eyes won't dry out."
Even blinks of the eye are registered.

As soon as she begins I want to do
everything I'm no longer allowed to do.
I want to scratch my ankle, clear my throat;
I want to take off my sweater, uncross
my legs. I want to sneeze. I want to go
down on some really hot guy, take his cock
deep inside my throat, feel it throb and jerk,
taste shot after shot of hot sticky cum
while my own cock shoots deep inside some smooth
stranger's ass as he writhes and cries for more.
I want it to be with Michael again;
want to cry out, "I love you. I miss you."

"Too much eye movement"—her voice from nowhere—
"Are you okay in there? We'll have to throw
this one out. You sure you're doing all right?"

I have to remember, the procedure's
simple: do not do what you have always done.

Watching "Destry Rides Again"

Yesterday you got the call
that Charlie died in New York.
I was watching Marlene
die, shot by her ex-lover.
Your body crumpled with hers.
At first I laughed, thinking you
were imitating Frenchie.
Then I noticed your face change—
the way your eyes had emptied,
the color gone from your cheeks.
There was no way to hold you.
You threw your glass on the floor
and screamed, "This isn't supposed
to be hap'ning! Not to us!"

This morning I watch you wake.
You wake up slowly. Your eyes
flutter. Your arm stretches out
in the bedside air. You raise
yourself up on one elbow,
mumble something like "mornin'."

We put the movie back in.
You want to see the ending.
"It's so beautiful," you say,
"the way she dies so slowly
in somebody else's arms.
That's the way I want to die."

You and I sit silently,
stare at the television.
Charlie dead at twenty-six
alone in his apartment.
The townspeople come to love
Destry as one of their own.
I remember your waking,
how I claimed you as my own.

REGINALD SHEPHERD

Born in New York City in 1963, Reginald Shepherd grew up in housing projects and tenements in the Bronx. Shepherd attended Brown University and the University of Iowa, where he earned graduate degrees in creative writing. He was the 1994–1995 Amy Lowell Traveling Scholar and now lives in Chicago. He is the author of two collections of poems, Some Are Drowning, *which was the winner of the 1993 Associated Writing Program Award in Poetry, and* Angel, Interrupted. *"These poems constitute an argument with the Romantic notion that, in Stevens's words, 'Death is the mother of beauty.' Such an idea remains true only when it remains metaphorical, within the death-like precincts of the ageless artwork. AIDS—as has been said so often as to make the assertion itself a metaphor—is no metaphor. It forces one to question the adequacy of metaphor (and thus of poetry) itself, if only for never having saved anyone: even oneself."*

Kindertotenlieder

After midnight everything becomes musical
like the names of flowers: names of diseases, for
example, like pneumocystis

carinii pneumonia blossoming in your lungs,
its petals of infection closing the breath. I wouldn't want
to make that beautiful, a self-congratulating sadness

in my blood. There are numbers of flowers
suitable for funerals whose names I don't know, many
of them toxic if ingested. Rinse the affected area

thoroughly with cold water, irrigate
the blood: surely something will grow there, something
has to. The body is surely no grave. Like

Kaposi's sarcoma, harsh syllables pronounced
across the skin, the purple lesions almost
hyacinth. No death is quite so flower-like, the god (who was

in love, remember) turning away so not to spoil the composition.
From that boy's blood a single flower sprang; the gardens
of Adonis wither within a week. I hate

the stupid flowers stealing youth. Beauty
is not an infection, contagion is no bloom upon the cheek, the thorn
that takes the rose into the true. The death

of beauty is diagnosed by no flower. How afraid I am
of your outstretched hand, its petals
white and black and falling fingers.

A Plague for Kit Marlowe

In Memory of Derek Jarman: "I place a delphinium, Blue, upon your grave."

I

I don't trust beauty anymore, when will I stop
believing it, repeating wilted petals? He loves
me not. Delphinium, cornflower, lupine, flowers
I've never seen; forget-me-not, fringed gentian,
lobelia, love-in-a-mist, old names of a world
that never was mine, the last of England's green
and pleasant island, sheer blue above the whited
Dover cliffs. Blue fog spelled out across an August sky
the blinded retina keeps, blue frost of a February
dawn, blue hour where you're dead. Agapanthus, also
called lily-of-the-Nile, closer to my lost continent. Pressed
in this anthology of hours, the serifed letters keep
for years of pages, film on water. Scilla, flax, large periwinkle.
Nothing is wasted but regret. Bluebell, blue flag.

II

The gardens of Adonis wither like burnt pages. Beauty
is an infection, I see now, the paper-thin skin written on water
like hyacinth, lily and anemone floating to decay. The filmy blossoms
fall apart like my hands, like *shallow rivers to whose falls
Melodious birds sing madrigals.* Narcissus was pushed, drowned in
a flood of song; Leander's white shoulder is coral echoing
in the Dardanelles. *For in his looks were all that men desire.*

I tramp through a closed garden of cures, Foscarnet, Retrovir,
Zovirax, pluck gaudy bouquets which wilt expensively
before ever reaching you. Roferon, Sporonox,
Leukine and Cytovene: those plastic flowers lose color
in the windows of a funeral home, pink wax and wire
accumulating dust like any dead. *And I will make thee
beds of roses And a thousand fragrant posies.*

III

Saw ye him whom my soul loveth? Will culture cure me, keep me
from harm? It let him die. I wanted some white immortality,
but find *I from myself am banish'd* in these lines, ghost body
of the light I poured away. My hands are stained and helpless
here, black ink spilled uselessly as any blood. The heart
is attached to a branching tree of capillaries, veins and arteries,
oxygen flowering like amaryllis, rose of Sharon, vermilion trumpets
forced in January, Sebastian's month. *Why should you love him
whom the world hates so?* The heart wants to keep opening
for seven years of any kind of luck, for any body's blood. Small bells
of paperwhite narcissus fill someone's winter with an idea of scent,
released of color, shape, or sense of touch. Who wouldn't wish
to linger in the sensual world that won't spare me, or let me hold
a living hand to him, *the king in whose bosom let me die.*

IV

I wanted something musical for you, notes floating
on the margins of a stranger's days and works: a lark, an air
of spring somewhere, my voice not clouded under error
just this once. How fine the song I wanted then,
changing from major to minor and, strangely,
back again. The knowing gods must think so little
of my minor wishes, all the sentimental tunes

I've memorized off-key: repeating every error helplessly
to make a song's my one refrain. I suppose I die
a little every day, not noticing it yet. I'm gathering dust
from an occasional shaft of light, I'm dotting all the i's
whole notes repeat, like why or cry. There's no finer tune
than afternoons clouded with luck all spring, the margin of error
I'd call a song. This happens every time I try to say goodbye.

RICHARD TAYSON

Born in California in 1962, Richard Tayson now lives in New York City. His poems have appeared in numerous magazines, including The Paris Review, Art & Understanding, *and* The Kenyon Review, *and he is the co-author (with Julia Tavalaro) of the book,* Look Up for Yes.

Blood Test

As the needle goes into my arm
I think of the moment
we first got into bed together:
your body prone along mine,
your shaved head against
my ribs. I kiss the stubble,
think how your anger
is the only thing you have left
as your body fails, blood cell
by blood cell. The nurse
fingers my pulse, asks
if I have nightsweats, any
unhealed marks on my body
and when I say no, I
hear your question as you
reach for the extra-strong
condoms on the table. You
hover over me, I
feel your swelling between my
thighs, you could
tear my inner membranes, expose
my blood to your own and
when I say no, you
want me to say it
again and again, your eyes
closing as you fling your
seed across my body until
I hear the nurse say she's
going to take the needle
out of my arm, straight
out of me. She's
quick to place the round
of cotton over the opening
and I think of the coin
placed over the eyes of the

dead. I
see the white drops of your
sperm on my stomach, watch
as your eyes open and
you see that I want it
off my body. You wet your
fingertips with the glutinous
fluid, shake them in my
face, saying *this is it, man,*
the only life we have now.

Peschanka

(The Russian town near what is now Volgograd,
where the German Sixth Army lost the battle of Stalingrad
in the winter of 1943, and 250,000 soldiers died.)

I read about the man who stood
50 years after the battle and saw
the field of human skeletons.
He bent close to the loamy earth
and took the photograph of one
skull, scream of the open
mouth, jaw-bone
broken, left molar
missing, and when I look up,
you sleep beside the open window.
You are letting the sun in, spring
in, your mouth open
against the ocher grain of the easy
chair, and suddenly you are not
breathing. I
put the magazine down, go to you and
touch your knee, when you do not
wake, I reach up, press
my hand to your mouth, as one who
wants to save another the torture
of slow death will place the pillow
over his face and press down
gently. I want to be
merciful, as I was told God is
merciful, I want to say *lie down*
my love in the green pasture, and

then I feel the gold silk of your
breath on my palm, and in my joy
I close the window, as if finally
locking the heavy cathedral
door. I touch
your shaved head, the stubble
pliant as grass shoots pressing
up through your skull, I press your
mouth to mine, and you
breathe, it's
summer, the fever
takes you and beats you, as the man
in the photograph was taken and
beaten and left to die.

The End

I have heard of the man
whispering into his dying
lover's ear, because the hearing
is the last to go, but now
that you walk into the living room
and turn on the compact disc player,
it's hard to remember
your body is undoing itself cell
by cell towards the time when
I will hold your head
erect, my hand along the proud
dome where your hair has fallen out,
pull you toward me and part
your lips with the spoon,
slide it past your teeth
and over your tongue, coaxing
the food down with some words,
some shorthand: *Corfu and cucumbers,*
which means think of the beach
where the naked man gave us
cucumbers and a ride in his boat
each day at 3. But now
you wait for the music,
and even with the weight loss
you look like the man I've always

loved, from the silver hair
and the wide nose, to the seven
pathetic chest hairs, down to the
mole on your left testicle,
right down to the anger.
I forgive that now, the broken
glass and the boiling water,
I forgive the affairs,
now that I know what your father
did to you. You wait hunched over
the disc player as one bends over
a fire in the cold, in the woods,
and when your favorite nocturne
begins, your neck muscles
relax, you turn
without fear to me and I
think what it will be like
when the feces come from you
like volcanic stone and I ask
the nurse to leave
and turn you onto your stomach,
coaxing, my hands
feeling your ribs and shoulder blades
as if the skin is no longer there—
and I take the sponge,
clean you off
until your shank flesh and buttocks
shine. But today
you come to me and I take you
in my arms, as a joyous man
will take his own brother father lover
into his arms. I wonder
who will clean me off if you
go first, the beginning and the end
being the same, really,
the one who is already here
helping the one to cross over from the other
side, the one remaining helping
the dying back across, holding on, listening.

In Sickness and in Health

For a week you lie beneath one sheet,
the fever comes, your face
darkens, the way a boy's face will
flush, the forehead hairs
dampen when his father comes at him
with a fire prod. Then the chill
comes, you sleep
beneath five blankets, your body
shaking, as a boy will freeze and
crack along a fracture line
when his parents lock him out
on the coldest night of the year.
Your head rests heavily on the pillow,
your face pale then bright
with the pink blooms like bruises
and I know you were a boy whose father
struck him with whatever was handy—
a rifle butt, a baseball bat,
a brick, once—
and I lift the blankets
as if parting the veil that separates
us from the next world. I touch
your underwear, checking for wetness,
smell your urine on my fingers
sweet as the life still in you,
slide the cloth down
your skinny hips and skinny legs,
take the sponge from the bowl
and clean you off. I wipe
the sticky sweet from your penis,
see how shrivelled and clammy the skin is,
how the tiny hairs are braided
together, curled
as if frozen beneath
ice and I
come even closer, see the pink
flush of the head, the greenish
web of veins on your thighs, the
mole on your left ball.
I think how many times
you have wanted me to explore your

body, in love, and I
dry you off, pull up
a fresh pair of underwear, climb
into bed beside you. I press my
clothed body against your ribs,
shoulders, your fine intelligent face
with the nose I've come to love
despite its imperfection, I
feel your eyelids flutter
beneath my fingers
as you wake for the first time
in two days and I kiss
your forehead and dirty
silver hair, comb out
the knots, your whole life
opening in the room.

JEAN VALENTINE

Born in Chicago, Jean Valentine has lived most of her life in New York City, where she has taught at Sarah Lawrence College. She is the author of seven collections of poems, including Dream Barker, The Messenger, Home Deep Blue: New and Selected Poems, *and, most recently,* Growing Darkness, Growing Light. *She now divides her time between New York and County Sligo, Ireland. She writes: "Knowing people with AIDS and their partners and families and friends has brought me closer to the campfire."*

To the Memory of David Kalstone

Here's the letter I wrote,
and the ghost letter, underneath—
that's my work in life.

The Night of Wally's Service, Wally Said,

"Most people will reflect back to you
however they feel about themselves,
but you have to say Hey,
Don't look at me that way,
I'm only one day dead,
I need care.
          But not Mark,
who looks at you with love.
No matter what. Like today, in church,
I was off somewhere, off Provincetown,
most people wanted me to come back,
but not Mark."

MAGGIE VALENTINE

Maggie Valentine lives in Providence, where she works with Rhode Island Project AIDS. "In 1988, my poems were filled with images of the sea, the seasons, beasts and birds, and the mild melancholy of solitude," she writes. "Then, for many reasons, I found myself deeply involved with AIDS. My more recent work has been informed by the spirit that often burns like a gas jet in people who are infected: it is more full of 'blood,' warmer, longer, peopled. It isn't only one's poetry that is changed."

William's Tale: The King of AIDS

When they start the morphine drip, Jon drifts
into his empire, into woods he wandered once,
woods frosted with shad-blossom that seems

to take a deep breath before it decides to bloom,
into a darkness lit by the strange shine
of his unreadiness to die;

a tree stump sprouting its own reincarnation
is his crown, gemmed with emerald,
dropped carelessly beside him in this tent of safety,

far from the epidemic, inhabited by the smaller angels.
He sits very straight on his throne, the tables

all around him covered with the gold of gifts
of flowers, his hoard of vials and boxes.
From where I sit, beside the bed, among

the get-well cards, the kidney pan, the polyester plant,
I see him grow translucent, a cut white tulip
left too long in water. I have said goodbye

more than once, I have grieved for him, only to have
a derelict angel's magic bring him back again,
all Kaposi's sarcoma and thrush, until, exhausted,

my heart broken against the implacable
hardness of it, I wish him gone, once and for all.

But next day Jon's awake, empty and full of wants:
He wants jewelry, "I want crystals, William," and "I want
you to buy me a ring, William," and "I want my robe

to be buried in, I want my cheeseburger, I wanted
chicken soup," and—offering me
a hospital spoon and a bowl of hospital Jello—

"Feed me, William."
He's supposed to stay in bed and not be trouble,
but a ferocious grace drives him

through all the fevers and ungodly smells and tests
that plague his 70 pounds; he hangs on to his life

so, there's nothing for it but to sign him out
—a costume for the masquerade ball—
and take him shopping.

He's hungry, no king was ever so hungry.
It gives him a thievish courage he turns
into the radical advocacy of self:

He steals from the market and the junk jewelry store,
hides his loot in his baseball jacket, in the pockets
of his wheelchair, looks pathetic, tells lies.

No monarch in history would ever have known such need,
it's worse than the need for bread:

He steals me from myself and eats me.
I could strangle him.
But every day we start again, I go down that hall

to see him, and something I love has happened again:
he has been touched
with a random royalty after all,

so that he sits in his bed,
bone-thin, demanding, tattooed
with the purple seal of his kingdom,

wearing the crown of the selfishness of the dying-young
like a divine right.

BELLE WARING

A poet and nurse, Belle Waring lives in Washington, D.C., where she teaches creative writing at Children's Hospital. Her first collection of poems, Refuge, was the winner of the 1989 Associated Writing Programs Award in Poetry and the 1991 Washington Prize. She writes: "Other than providing the obvious subject—apocalypse—the influence of AIDS on my work is something I cannot rightly tease out from its influence on my character. Of my fury toward the American government's response to the pandemic, I won't speak, but rather I will honor the late Sony Labou Tansi, who wrote this before he died of AIDS: 'To be a poet nowadays is to want to ensure, with all one's body and with all one's soul, that in the face of guns, in the face of money (which in its turn becomes a gun), and above all in the face of received wisdom (upon which we poets have the authority to piss), no aspect of human reality is swept into the silence of history.' "

Baby Random

tries a nosedive, kamikaze,
when the intern flings open the isolette.

The kid almost hits the floor. I can see the headline:
DOC DUMPS AIDS TOT. Nice save, nurse,

Why thanks. Young physician: "We have to change
his tube." His voice trembles, six weeks

out of school. I tell him: "Keep it to a handshake,
you'll be OK." Our team resuscitated

this Baby Random, birth weight
one pound, eyelids still fused. Mother's

a junkie with HIV. Never named him.
Where I work we bring back terminal preemies,

No Fetus Can Beat Us. That's our motto. I have
a friend who was thrown into prison. Where do birds

go when they die? Neruda wanted to know. Crows
eat them. Bird heaven? Imagine the racket.

When Random cries, petit fish on shore, nothing
squeaks past the tube down his pipe. His ventilator's

a high-tech bellows that kicks in & out. Not
up to the nurses. Quiet: a pigeon's outside,

color of graham crackers, throat oil on a wet street,
wings spattered white, perched out of the rain.

I have friends who were thrown in prison, Latin
American. Tortured. Exiled. Some people have

courage. Some people have heart. *Corazon.*
After a shift like tonight, I have the usual

bad dreams. Some days I avoid my reflection in store
windows. I just don't want anyone to look at me.

So What Would You Have Done?

On the train to D.C., a priest sat beside me, and outside Phillie
he turned and said *My daughter has only days to live.*

Rawboned man. Under his eyes were purple crescents
like bruises dug out by a surgeon's thumb.

He wept, I was scared, but not for myself.
Of course, for myself.

I took his hand then—cold as inside of a limestone chapel.
Wilmington next.

He pressed both my hands before he left. I wanted him please
to bless me again, bless the train and the tracks for they could snap like

fingers like the string of smoky pearls my sweetheart gave to me
before he got sick.

           Before they admitted him.
One day, on my way to the hospital, I saw some movers drop a baby grand—

it broke from its harness to the street.
One honors the chord of a crashed piano by scrounging ivory

for a charm.
There is logic in this.

                  When I walked into my sweetheart's room,
I saw the chemo had gotten to his scalp. He was ripping out

handfuls of his own hair, black dandelion seedfluff, saying,
Take it. It doesn't even hurt.

I wound his hair round the shard of ivory to conjure the elephant to save him—
but later, I didn't tell the priest I had a charm in my pocket.

After Wilmington, after he left, a teenaged boy with a ripped leather jacket
took the same seat, still warm.

He looked at me staunchly: *You all right?*
I said, *My boyfriend's dead.*

Kid gave me a cigarette.
I showed the charm to him and he said

I should give it to my Mom to keep my Dad off her.
Crossing the Severn, he fell asleep, twitching in a dream.

High arched brows. Eyes chasing, or being chased.
I unwound from the charm the black hair of my boyfriend,

and wrapped my own hair around it, to slip in the kid's pocket.
There was a pistol in it.

                  The train cut close by suburban yards
where cars roosted up on blocks, an upside-down dory perched like a hen

warming herself in the sun-shot dirt, a kid climbing into a tulip poplar
tore off whole blossoms to toss to his mother

as dusty babies swarmed on the grass below.
They never looked up.

All I wanted was to hear them, please
                            calling each other.

For My Third Cousin Ray John

I poured salt on slugs when I was a kid.
Foaming, they died while I watched with the thuggish
delight of a child—slight savage.
It was Ray John taught me. Two, we two
in our garbled kinhood, awash, 1956.
A small town is a boat that the wind makes a toy,
boat in a foam sea, oh the tinderbox terror of it.
Daddy's killing Mama again. What is
the impulse to save? You slugs, your killer confesses
to murder quite plain. Why was it fun?

I had to hide Ray John. The secret was
we were in the long grass. The secret now is
Ray John will die of AIDS, and soon. This
I've never told because he hurts. Me, I refuse
to bear the cross in the eyes of the nurse
who spits in the sink when I'm not looking. Looking
is something I do not enjoy. Look, any soul will do—
take mine. Because Ray John
is a better item than me or his parents.
They should be the dead ones—

> take me,
> not him.

I shouldn't have let him go down in that culvert when we were kids—
lie, dash, get a kiss. Away from Mama. I would save him.
Who knows where the virus diddles.
I would draw the poison as salt pulls fluid
where the wild grass grows up to cover us.
Ray John, without the dogs they'll never find us.
Lie down and pretend you're the grass of the field, Ray John,
don't cry 'cause the devil can't catch us

> *Where the workers of iniquity flourish*
> *they shall be cut down*
> *and the righteous shall grow as the cedar of Lebanon*

because I'll come back to you, never worry.
I will come right to you—
when have I not been with you—
I will lie down with you and cover you
and I will carry you into the dark dark finish

MARVIN K. WHITE

Marvin K. White's poems have appeared in such anthologies as The Road Before Us: 100 Gay Black Poets; Sojourner: Black Gay Voices in the Age of AIDS; *and* Gents, Bad Boys, and Barbarians: New Gay Male Writing. *He lives in Oakland, California, and organizes performance events in the Bay Area. "It has become important," he writes, "that I publish and present more poetry for fear that neither family nor history will do me justice. I know too many black gay poets whose work has been buried or burned with them, never to surface again."*

Last Rights

When I learned of Gregory's death
I cried silently
but at the funeral
giiiiirl I'm telling you
I rocked Miss Church
hell I fell to my knees twice
before I reached my seat
three people had to carry me
to my pew
I swayed and swooned
blew my nose
on any and every available sleeve
the snot was flying everywhere
then when I finally saw his body
my body jerked itself
right inside that casket
and when I placed my lips on his
honey the place was shaking
I returned to my seat
but not before passing by his mother
who I'm sure at this point
was through with me
I threw myself on her knees
shouting, "Help me,
help me Jesus"
when someone in the choir
sang out, "Work it girl,
wooooork it"
all hell broke loose
I was carried out
kicking and screaming
ushered into the waiting limo

which sped me to his family's house
where I feasted
on fried chicken
hot water corn bread
macaroni and cheese
Johnnie Walker Black
finally in my rightful place

That Thing

He still singing in the choir
he still loving men
he still kiki-ing at the club
he still sometimes real still

He got that thing
that Magic Johnson got
that Arthur Ashe had
that Easy-E had
that Ryan White had
but he's never been a basketball star
tennis ace
rapper
or little white boy

That thing
forces his knuckles through his skin
ashes his oils as dry as driftwood
Pulls his face too close to his skull
brings his eyes back into his head
now he can finally see what
he's been thinking

and those purple, blue and black spots
aren't bruises he can excuse away

cuz it ain't like that thing
he got in high school then college
this thing and that thing
as different as he is now
but he told me it still burns
more like freezing
less like fire

and he's thinking about
slitting his wrists
because he knows he's
bleeding to death anyway

He still singing in the choir
he still loving men
he still kiki-ing at the club
he still sometimes real still

He got that thing
and he stopped looking
for all the same differences
in his body
he stopped remembering
forgotten and torn condoms
he stopped remembering
the highs and the lows
the raw and the rips
in his skin

He got that thing
and he told his mama
he got that thing
and so now she takin' care
of her thing and that thing

He got that thing
from his friend
from being smart enough
to sell his body
when he was in prison
when he was in the hospital
when he was in the bushes
and through the red cracked
skin of lips
he says he gonna be all right

He still singing in the choir
he still loving men
he still kiki-ing at the club
he still sometimes real still

DONALD W. WOODS

The son of Barbadian immigrants, Donald W. Woods was born in 1957 and grew up in New York City, where he studied poetry with Audre Lorde and music with Ysaye Barnwell, and where he was active in the Blackheart Collective and Other Countries. As the Executive Director of AIDSFILMS, he developed two AIDS preventions videos, Reunion *and* Party, *aimed at black gay men. He was the author of* The Space, *a portfolio of poems whose publication was supported by Art Matters, Inc., and his poems appeared in* In the Life: A Black Gay Anthology *and* Sojourner: Black Gay Voices in the Age of AIDS; *he himself appears in Marlon Riggs's film* Non, Je Ne Regrette Rien. *He died of AIDS-related complications in June 1992, at the age of thirty-five.*

Waiting

my feet mark the passage of time
i leave off where i started
the hospital
fingering my toes

in time i am healthy
robust waiting
for the light
humming waiting

bells toll
in slow solid measures
the bolt that connects my arm whispers
and the way i sweat
in bursts and starts
in increments
i talk in measures
if and when
plan in yardsticks
less than three feet long
i will go to the wedding
the graduation is a wait and see
see and wait
for the light at sixth and somewhere
ten years past the flirting muslims
if i wait my prince will come
it's a promise
the way stars twinkle
the way light bursts against the back of your lids

when pain beats your ass with short stabs
lower pelvic pain
you tell the doctor who has waited all day
for his favorite patient
with my meditation walkman
well, peaceful and happy
i am still hopeful waiting

on the corner of sixth and something
i am breathing deep through my mouth
exhaling through wide nostrils
i am tired of waiting
the passage the ritual the long ride sitting
'cross from someone who never cries
weary of listening to my beathing
when i don't know what to listen for
when am i massaging the feet of death itself
searching with confident fingers for the corollary
between the sole and the soul's song
singing at the bedside of another brother
who will sing for me
who sings for me now
where is that man the muslims promised
the messiah of love
the self-healed herald of our age
always waiting
told bert that and he
remembered recalled it aloud
as i waited for
a train—a bus—a man
he said "i know how you hate to wait"
and smiled at me

breathing measuring sweating
sniffing at the feet of death
my hands anointed by their own work
my prayers and poems a tangled mass
of flashing lights and signals
waiting for themselves to unlock the
lazarus the job the mary virgin mystery
why me they cried and waited
watching my children grow
my waistline shrink

in measures and increments
research on mice and monkeys
lipstick stains a thousand paper cups
the amusement park opens then closes
the season ended
the kids overdressed for school
wait for the crossing guard in her reflector vest
she signals to them and they cross
at sixth and somehow
time stands still for them
i wait for it to resume
the hairs on my neck
the clearing of my throat
helps me to measure
the time that belongs to me
time left over
minutes left out of the scheme
of waiting patient
if i wait here patient it will happen

i will die
crashing noiselessly into my own consciousness
pillows of waiting of sickness of health
featherbed of lingering near the edges
waiting for my change to come
cushions of sorrow and regret
catch my nose dive my dead weight
plummet by here in a minute
you'll see soar past your dead weight fall
pouring my living into a glass of bubbles
their iridescence is reflective
but i can't get caught in the mirror on the way
the way waiting has no end
the way waiting makes you wait
listening makes you listen
and your ideas don't solve the puzzle
your ideas are not in this
it's you and me who hates to wait
it's me and you waiting for this weight i lost
no one understood that
his peeling his bound feet his cranky whining
were mine his limp rag suffering tubes and tracheotomies
boiler plate passages indexed in our
mutual living

burning oxygen together was a pleasure
heaving and spewing stories to pass the time
the time the time the clock
spring forward fall back
lose an hour or what
gain a day by waiting quiet
lose a week by running scared
filling the book with precious appointments
talking in measured tones
lean against the buzzer
lean against the buzzer
and wait for the time to come

MARK WUNDERLICH

Mark Wunderlich is currently a Fellow at the Fine Arts Work Center in Provincetown, Massachusetts. His poems have appeared in such magazines as Poetry, The Paris Review, *and* The Yale Review. *"My first memory of any reference to AIDS was as an adolescent growing up in rural Wisconsin," he writes. "A childhood friend of my father's—a man I remember being talked about in hushed tones and with great judgment—had died at a young age. I could tell that the element of secrecy and shame linked to the death of this man was something I would have to contend with. As a gay man who has come of age since the AIDS crisis began, the disease has always been a presence in my sexual and emotional life. By choosing to write about sexuality, it has been necessary to address the impact of the disease on my world."*

The Bruise of This

The night I woke to find the sheets wet from you,
like a man cast up on the beach,
I hurried you off to the shower to cool you down,

dressed you, the garments strict and awkward in my hands,
and got you into a taxi to the hospital,
the driver eyeing us from the slim disk of his mirror—

The blue tone of the paging bell,
the green smocks, metal beds,
plastic chairs linked
in a childhood diagram of infection,

and when they wheeled you by
there was a needle in your arm,
the bruise of this
already showing itself,

and rather than watch gloved doctors handle you
in their astonishing white coats and crisp ties,
I took a seat outside and waited,
time yawning out, white and static—

a hallway, a bedsheet—
and made clear to me in the bright light of speculation
was time's obstacle in the body,
and those things I could do that might cushion it.

How I Was Told and Not Told

There was the milky sun washing out the sky
and his hair fanned out on the pillow above
the drunk and muscled crush of him.

In the room, the night had left its mark—
ashes in a saucer, burning amber in a glass,
the slow ribbon of news slipping out.

The husk of his voice hangs
in the morning air, and outside
the wind starts its hurling.

Left lingering, a fossil,
is the shape of him
in the empty bed.

*   *   *

The needle punctures the vein
to consider the blood. No trace left
of the body's perfect red moon.

I am alarmed by the weight of objects
and the way light is consumed
by the greedy sky. In sleep

I have already heard the ruffling of papers
the dry movements of insects,
the tray of utensils' bright

clatter and chime.
I lay down my want of him
like a lock of hair in a cedar box

and the moon with its bone sliver
and loose stitches of black
bastes up the night sky.

JOEL ZIZIK

Joel Zizik was born in El Paso, Texas, in 1963, and earned his M.A. in Creative Writing from the University of Texas at El Paso, where he also taught part-time; he died, by suicide, in 1993, when he was thirty. His first collection of poems, Hypoglycemia and the Need to Practice It, *was published shortly after his death.*

Pneumocystis

to Fred Nogales, Fall 1992

You had to tell your parents
each part of France and what they grow there.

As they drove you to the airport,
your hands pretended to hold the wheel.

The air on the plane was drier than the air of El Paso.

Your lips began to crease with tiny lines.

It took three flights to get to Paris,
the last one became
a kind of motel room for everyone,
the normal urban silence abandoned for a few hours.

You took off your shoes and wanted to walk around the cabin.

After a while, the water underneath you made no sense.

*   *   *   *

Ah, those Frenchmen,
the yellow pallor of their skin
was a revelation to you.
Their fingers seemed to have no extra flesh.

You wanted to touch the linen shirts
they wore every day,
even Saturday mornings.

You told them you were from Mexico.

Do you ever think of their dying now,
their confusion in the narrow streets of Paris,
their bodies opening and closing each new illness?

Of one of them in particular telling his parents?

Did one of them ever try to call you,
thinking you were somewhere in Mexico?

*   *   *   *

Maybe you saw him on the street, in a bar,

maybe he was eating expensive food by himself.

Eventually, you saw something vivid in him,
and he put his hands on your hair.

Then happiness sleeved open to have you.

In those days, the early Eighties, it must have been so remote,

a death that would feel like stone
for a while, and then like tooth,
and then like a strong wind.

In those days, it would have been flattering
to say, Yes,

drop yourself into me as finally
as a coffin being lowered down on rough cords.

*   *   *   *

After making love,
you wondered how you ended up in Paris,
so giant over its own dark river.

The next time you went to the Louvre,
did you notice Delacroix,

the Christs, dying, deflated,
relieved to be on their way,

their flesh finally drained of conflict,

their faces like fields of soft, exhausted blossoms,

their strong pronouncements of jaw?

Is the story of Jesus any sadder
if you think he was beautiful,
if you think he gave up a life of ardor
and madness and disappeared forever?

*   *   *   *

I moved to New York in 1983,
the last year of the Seventies, they say.

I met someone from upstate.

I met his boyfriend,
the man he had moved to the city with,
who couldn't stop coughing.

One night, they showed me
the very western edge of West 14th street,
the abandoned packing houses,
the rooms of men
at the end of a long, long day.

My friends said, *Just walk in,*
you know what will happen,
someone will start to touch you.

But I could hear breathing noises
from the doorway, sounds of suffocation.

So we sat on a pier pointing away from the city.

I moved back to El Paso less than a year later.

When I went to New York in 1987,
someone else was in their apartment,
and no one remembered them at their jobs.

*   *   *   *

When we met, Fred, in 1988,
we only had stories.

You told me how you had to pick tomatoes,
for a while, in the south of France,
the only thing you could do without papers.

As you spoke, your chest moved in and out.

You were back in your own wide language.

I put my head on your sternum and listened.

I talked about school,
the daily injustices of work.

The slope of your shoulder
made a little cradle for my head.

Now I think, still, after all,
what is love, what can it ever be,
but its willful gestures of retention?

*   *   *   *

A year after we met, you began to recede.

The referential smile started dimming at the table,

the languages going, stem by stem,

the place between your skin
and your pleasure at having skin,

everything that announced you,

getting briefer.

The civilization of your laughter.

You hardly spoke.

I didn't understand, I didn't think of a virus,
I thought you were tiring of me.

When I broke up, I wrote you a letter
saying our love had no perfect examples.

A month later, I would remember the men in your culture,

the cancer plain on your father's face,

and how he never said a word or ever saw a doctor.

*   *   *   *

I was out of town the first time you almost died.

I had seen you lying down for days before I left,

your breathing fast and attenuated,

the fever rising until you were liquid
inside your skin, like a small, young planet,

and I left anyway.

105°, it turned out,
when someone finally took you to the hospital
and you went blind for most of an afternoon.

The boy who sat next to me in second grade
died of pneumonia, double pneumonia,
during the first month of school,

but we were there,
in church on a Tuesday evening, to pray for him.

*   *   *   *

It hit us both at the same time,
the same day, in fact,
in our different cities:

the loss of weight, the fever,
the way school had grown more and more important to you.

Those six months in Paris.

When I called you,
your family said something about bronchitis.

At that time of year,
the afternoons are very similar.

I called once a day, sometimes in the evening.

For seven days in a row,
they said you were fine
but could not come to the phone.

*   *   *   *

After I came back, I took my place
in the small chorus around your bed.

You lay there, three weeks in the hospital,

afternoons so quiet
you could hear the low long unbroken *ah* of not existing
getting ready inside you.

You travelled back and forth between worlds,
between what you had
and a sharp wanting,

your chosen death, whatever it was,
stripped from you.

This is one of those diseases
that make you love the world, suddenly,
and then slowly tell you
your love for this world is not enough.

*   *   *   *

At first, I thought your suffering was mostly deprivation,

the foods that had become poisonous,

the places you couldn't go
because neuropathy had put your foot to sleep,

the wondering
where one long continuous driving of your body might take you,

if the length of your health were completely random.

One day, I watched the news
with you and listened to your reactions.

I saw your suffering become ideology.

I think I told myself, *like everyone else*,

and then I heard you ask the nurse
if it was safe to drink the tap water.

And then I tried to believe
there was mysterious information in your agony.

*   *   *   *

Suddenly, in the middle of your recovery,
my own test results came back from the lab.

When I went to get them,
I took four hundred dollars in my pocket.

As I sat in the waiting room,
the wind rose, from time to time,
and lifted something in the parking lot,
a scrap of cloth or important paper.

I smelled a strong, unbearable sweetness in my hair,

I tasted something in my mouth,
not the ordinary taste of my own life.

People had told me
this kind of love would lead to death.

202 • Joel Zizik

They probably didn't mean a withering inside me.

*   *   *   *

The nurse said,
The acidity in your mouth has saved your life.
If you love him,
tell him you're negative before he dies.

As I walked into your hospital room,
ready to tell you,

I remembered all the Sexton
I had read to you before we knew you were infected,

when the virus was still deciding what it would do in you,

back before the last of your life was activated.

Over and over I'd told you the story
of my father shooting himself in his car,

of my sister shooting herself five years later
with my other sister listening on the phone.

I had told you, over and over,
that I wanted to die just like them.

*   *   *   *

When my father shot himself in 1981,
I thought something like:

We are links in a process of existence
whose evolution is using each of our lives up.

And: *If you have no children,*
killing youself may be your only act of divinity,

transmit disgust for this world
and then move on,
your work is done.

When my sister shot herself,
I wanted a clear, deliberate death in spite of the fear.

Years later, I bought a shotgun,
I drove to the middle of the desert and sat down.

Then I started to think about the metal pellets,
the taste of the powder burning
for a second, in my mouth,
the tender, mucous suspension of the soft palate. . . .

Just turning of the safety took ten minutes of thinking.

I finally aimed at the vegetation, I squeezed my finger,

some round grey brush broke in two,
it seemed like, from the noise alone.

So now if I say, *I want to die,*
I know it will mean a process, a ritual of fear
and expelling fear that could take the whole afternoon.

*   *   *   *

And then there was the quilt, this year, in D.C.

I got there when they were still laying it out.

So I went to the Vietnam Wall, its long undulation
pulls you forward,
there's one graceful message of community.

Then I walked down the aisles of the quilt,

each banner different, a different kind of breath
gets stuck in you at each one.

Some of them had portraits, smiling,
the way they were smiling ten years ago.

Suddenly, again, for a second,
I wanted a death like theirs,
that described the accidental world.

I told myself, *If you go along,*
they'll all be waiting.
They'll put down their pencils and hold your face.

I stood still.

I think I wanted everyone on the nearby panels
to notice how sad, how irreparable
I seemed, in the middle of catastrophe,
with nowhere to go.

*   *   *   *

So now we wait.

Each time I call you, I listen for a lather
behind your voice.

Your lungs are becoming despondent in your body,

the air only lasts a few seconds in your blood.

Sometimes I have this dream
where you breathe louder and louder
until you drown in the last stage of your resolve.

Sometimes you butterfly the nervous system
open and dissolve as you hit the air.

And sometimes you die far away from your body—
whoever is pressed against your skin,
the context of your going,
he has access only to your gestures of refusal.

The flowers that arrive seem frozen
on their stems.

They say,

Whatever opens, opens into the world.

That is the nature of infection.

*   *   *   *

Now the doctors say,
when you want to make love,
there may only be a downward rush of blood
and sudden temperament,

a vague bristling.

Maybe you'll feel desire floating free,
itinerant in your body.

The man you love now
slowly takes rigidity from your hands.

You are superficial against his skin,
the way lovers are, at first, until boredom
leads them open-mouthed to the internal.

Intent is delivered by moths.

Pleasure recants slowly.

Then, for a while, you hold what you need
low in yourself, under your stomach sounds.

*   *   *   *

Fred, do you remember your dreams at fifteen,

your questions about the origin of this love for other men?

One night, your dream would tell you:
interrupt the patrilineage for fun.

The next night, it would suggest
an overwhelming tree had just been planted
by the people who owned your house before you.

There were dim narratives about money and love.

A man would come to you, his shirt loose, and say nothing.

You'd wake up.

Your hair felt like it started from deep bones.

Hmmmm

When Jay died, after a whole day of groaning,
I thanked god
the terrible commitment to live finally gets discouraged.

For a whole day, he had moaned, unconscious—

one loud, wild, unmistakable expression of pain,
each time he took a breath.

Other patients had begun to come out of their rooms,
what's wrong with him, what are they doing to him,

and then a priest showed up,
really out of nowhere,
I still don't know who called him.

He said,
I understand that Jay was . . .

and then he fluttered his flat, open hand back and forth,

the same gesture I have seen people use all my life
to mean mediocre, perverse, gay, crooked, crazy,

but he meant, *an atheist,*
or, *wavering in his commitment to a church,*

and he said, *which I can respect.*

He put his hands on Jay's chest
and then directly on the bulb of his forehead.

Think of the first hand that ever touched you
with the promise of love,
when it held your arm and you felt the body didn't matter.

He took Jay's body and offered it to someone who promised
to lift a beautiful thing out of it,

and solve the twin religious and artistic hatreds of waste.

Shortly after that,
the groaning sounded like it went from *help* to *no* to *hmmmm*.

Hmmmm, the noise of small surprises,

or like a monk chanting, hunting for something
deep in the bowl of the song.